A Man Like This

A Personal Reflection on the Thoughts of Bishop William Lee Bonner

James C. Richardson, Jr.

Broad Wing Press
Lanham, MD

A Man Like This

Copyright 2007 by James C. Richardson, J.

All rights reserved. No part of this book may be reproduced without permission in writing from the publisher or the author

© 2019 Broad Wing Press

ISBN 10: 1-938373-14-6

ISBN 13: 978-1-938373-14-5

Library of Congress Control Number: 2018965828

Printed in the United States of America

Table of Contents

Acknowledgements i

Preface 5

Chapter One

    Introduction 1

Chapter Two

    From the Plantation in Georgia to the Pulpit in New York 13

Chapter Three

    The Apostolic Dilemma 21

Chapter Four

    Women, Ministry, and the Church 39

Chapter Five

    What About Your Emotions? 73

Chapter Six

    The Holy Spirit: Another Comforter.......................... 95

Chapter Seven

    Armageddon 131

Conclusion

    Stay on Course 157

Bibliography 159

Appendices

    Churches Pastored by Pastor Bonner 163

    Board of Apostles (2006) 165

Acknowledgements

As with any project like this, there are vital contributions from others who selflessly assist in seeing it through to fruition. That has most certainly been the case here. In that regard, I must offer an abundance of thanks to my Mt. Sinai Writing Committee for so many hours of volunteer assistance.

To Mrs. Shermale Motley, your keen mind and editorial skills provided so many wise insights for the initial manuscript.

Also, to Ms. Nancy Perkins, thank you for working laboriously in transcribing much of my often-illegible writing. Somehow you managed to decipher my odd strokes that supposedly mean something in the English language. Additionally, your comprehensive knowledge of words, in general, leaves me wondering at your ability to spell almost any word correctly.

To Mrs. Carolyn M. Harris, I am deeply touched by your sense of commitment to the Lord's work. Two days after we celebrated the Homegoing of your late husband, Deacon Larry Harris, you were back in the office helping the committee to help me meet our deadline. Additionally, your amazing computer skills provided such a blessed contribution to the completion of this project.

Mrs. Mary Ann Mason, my natural sister and administrative assistant, they call you a "Senior Citizen." But your energy level seems to rise with each passing year in your life. Your willingness to evaluate and fill whatever position that is vacant to complete the task constantly amazes me. From childhood into what is now our senior years, you always find new ways to express your unconditional love for your "bro", Thank you for transcribing, editing, and anything else that I asked of you.

To the Mt. Sinai Church Family, so very much do I appreciate your patience and understanding as I sometimes seemed to meander through getting this project completed. Thank you for your prayers and support. I love all of you.

And finally, to my wife and partner "Lady Glo," thank you for listening to me discuss the book with you most evenings; and giving candid and helpful feedback. You know that I have always been grateful for your straightforwardness and stability in all things. Your discerning mind has helped and blessed me way too many times to count. I love you simply because you are you.

Preface

Words really are inadequate to express my appreciation to Chief Apostle William L. Bonner for agreeing to my doing this project; writing this book about him. It has truly been a labor of love.

For those who are a part of the Pentecostal-Apostolic tradition, I do hope that this book increases your knowledge about one of the most outstanding servants the Lord has in these contemporary times. And, for those who have very limited knowledge about us, I pray that reading about this gentle giant of a man will stimulate your desire to find out more about this segment of the vineyard in the Kingdom of God.

As the Lord would have it, Pastor Bonner was providentially placed in my life the same year my natural father transitioned. And the Bishop has provided for me such a sterling example of one who has totally surrendered his will to the Master's will.

All we need to do is follow the example that the Lord has enabled him to set before us. We have certainly discovered that our meager excuses don't hold very much water when you see the consistent dedication and commitment of a servant like Pastor Bonner.

My fervent prayer is that those of us who see what the Lord has deposited into him, will not allow complacency and apathy to be the barriers that stop us from achieving. Pastor Bonner's long example of the prayerful lifestyle shows us the powerful and tangible results with which the Lord will bless.

Oh, yes there will be burdens, but apparently, the blessings by far exceed any burdens that we may have to endure.

Again, my profound gratitude is conveyed to Pastor Bonner for his willingness to share information that he could easily have chosen not to divulge. And, in his sharing, I deeply appreciated his candor and forthrightness. But the humor that Pastor Bonner possesses is wonderfully refreshing while at the same time being unexpectedly disarming. Above all, I appreciate his total commitment and determination to do all that the Lord is calling him to do.

My chief apostle and pastor thank you; I love you!!!

Chapter One
Introduction

Bishop William Lee Bonner is, to say the least, an extraordinary human being. So many people who know him would use adjectives in the superlative in a meager attempt to describe Pastor Bonner, his preferred title.

Now those who appear to work closest with him either have some involvement in one of the five churches he pastors, or they hold positions in the Church of Our Lord Jesus Christ (COOLJC). My relationship with him though has developed outside of those two areas of his ministry. Instead, ours has evolved through my association with the W. L. Bonner College as a faculty member. This institution was founded in 1995 and received the first level of accreditation in 1999 by the Intonational Christian Accrediting Association (ICAA). The college is now in the final stages of also being accredited by The Association for Biblical Higher Education (ABHE). A key component of the ABHE is our recognition by the United States Department of Education. Because of this we now receive financial aid for our students.

With an affiliation with the Church of Our Lord Jesus Christ, WLBC is now a leading higher education institution among predominantly Black Apostolic Churches in the world. It is then our hope that a wider segment of Apostolics (Oneness Pentecostals) will start making application to join us on the campus in Columbia, SC.

Let me quickly add though that our faculty and student body are interdenominational and interracial. Thus, we invite students from all ethnic groups and religious affiliations (even no affiliation) to come have the WLBC experience. We truly believe that it will be unlike any other college. Well, I guess that concludes my "P.R." spot for WLBC.

In addition to our professional relationship, this association has given the opportunity for us to develop very meaningful and significant personal ties. To say the least, my wife, Gloria, and I, our church family and national organization love him immensely. Additionally, we have the highest respect and regard for Pastor Bonner.

Please allow me to share with you how I really met this wonderful servant of God. While living in Washington, DC (1971-1976), it was my privilege to hear his weekly broadcast every Saturday afternoon. Like so many others, I was a very faithful listener. Even on the radio, there was a special anointing that came through in a powerful way while this man of God ministered.

One Friday night, in the spring of 1975 (I believe) Pastor Bonner was scheduled to preach at the Holy Temple Church of Christ in southeast Washington, DC, with founding pastor, Bishop Joseph Weathers, whom I met a few years earlier when he was serving as an assistant to the late Bishop H. C. Brooks. Of course, Bishop Brooks was the founder of the Way of the Cross Church of Christ, and pastor of the mother church at 9th and D Streets, northeast Washington, DC.

My initial acquaintance with the Way of the Cross Organization came from Mt. Sinai's fellowship with the Shiloh Way of the Cross Church in Martinsville. The late Bishop H. C. Eggleston was the founding pastor, and he and my father were personal friends. Shiloh is now pastored by Bishop Earley Dillard. On the national level, Bishop Leroy Cannady, Baltimore, MD serves as the current presiding bishop. But Bishop Alphonso Brooks pastors the mother church in Washington, DC and he is the youngest son of the late H. C. Brooks.

Hearing that Pastor Bonner would be ministering at Holy Temple, a former seminary colleague, Dr. James Brooks and I decided to attend that service. (Dr. Brooks is now chairman of the Department of Philosophy and Religion at Bethune Cookman College, Daytona Beach, FL). Being young elders at the time, Brooks and I were totally surprised when we got to Holy Temple. We expected to be seated on the floor with the other youthful ministers, or even with the deacons. The pulpit would be reserved for the bishops and senior elders. To our shock, Bishop Weathers invited Brooks and me to the pulpit and upon his entering, Pastor Bonner came to each minister, greeted us personally, and took his seat. That was in 1975 and I have always been grateful to Bishop Weathers for extending that wonderful gesture of Christian hospitality.

Little did I know in 1975 the monumental difference that twenty years would make in my relationship with Bishop Bonner. You see, 1995 was the year that my father Bishop J. C. Richardson, Sr. transitioned from earth to glory; March 2nd, to be exact. After the passing of my father, there was such a sense of void in my life. Not only was I his namesake and sole son, but we also had a very close relationship. He was truly my mentor, and I loved him dearly. Whenever I had difficulty finding or rightly interpreting a scripture, I would call him. He would either immediately give me the answer or call me back within 15 minutes. The longest time it ever took him to respond to me was 30 minutes and that occurred only once.

At the time, Dad had served as founding pastor of our church Mount Sinai, for 60 years. He was also the co-founder (with Bishop 1. W. Audrey, Bishop J. J. Jenkins, Elder Willie Bryant, and Elder J. M. Williams) of the Apostle Church of Christ in God (ACCG) in 1941. And, from 1956-1995, served as our presiding bishop.

Dad's homegoing celebration was March 6, 1995. In May of 1995, the ACCG United Council met at the St. Matthew Apostolic Temple in Winston-Salem, NC, where Bishop Joseph P. Lowery is the pastor. During that Council, the ACCG Executive Board met to determine who the next spiritual and administrative leaders would be for the Apostle Church of Christ in God. As I recall the Elder

Joe N. Gravely, Jr. made the motion that I become the presiding bishop, that Bishop J. P. Lowery would become first vice bishop, and that Bishop Harry W. Betts, pastor of St. Luke Apostle Church in South Boston, VA, would become second vice bishop. The motion carried and was presented as a recommendation to the Assembly of Delegates, who overwhelmingly voted for ratification. The installation was scheduled to take place in the 1995 Holy Convocation at the Mt. Sinai Church.

Elder Joe N. Gravely, Jr. is no longer an official part of the ACCG, he is now an overseer in the World Assemblies of Restoration (WAR). Their presiding prelate is Bishop James Nelson from Baltimore, MD. But Elder Gravely is a son of Mt. Sinai having begun his preaching ministry under the tutelage of Bishop 1. C. Richardson, Sr. Additionally, his is still a close and much valued friendship.

As our thoughts began to turn toward the Convocation, the need to select a preacher for the special occasion became a high priority. In the fifty-four-year history of the ACCG, only two men had sat in the presider's chair. They were Bishop 1. W. Audrey 1941-1956, and Bishop J. C. Richardson, Sr. 1956-1995. What an awesome and humbling task that stood before Bishop Betts, Bishop Lowery and me. Immediately the entire Executive Board went into prayer seeking direction from the Lord as to who should come and minister. Because Dad has served as our presider for 39 years, he was the only one that the vast majority of the members had ever known. He was much beloved as a father and grandfather figure, in addition to being our presider.

What is so ironic is that during the deliberations by the Executive Board concerning possible preachers to come, Pastor Bonner's name never came up, because we were looking at two groups of ministers: either those who were close to my father or those who were close to me. Time was moving and we had not yet made a decision. One day in June 1995, as I rested in the bedroom at my home, I asked the Lord, "Who do you want me to get for this Convocation?" The answer came back, "Bishop William L. Bonner." Keep in mind now, I was not asleep. So, I asked again, "Who Lord?" Again, the response was "Bishop William L. Bonner." To say that my mind was filled with shock and total surprise would be an understatement.

At that time, my secretary was the late Sister Rubena (Ruby) King Lloyd. She had lived in New York over thirty years and served as the administrative assistant to the superintendent of schools in New Rochelle. When she and her husband Leonard retired, they moved back to her hometown of Martinsville. While in New York, she attended the Strait Gate Church in Mamaroneck, NY then pastored by the late Bishop Alfred Powell. It is now pastored by his son, Dr. Wayne Powell,

Based on the connections of Sister Lloyd and mine, we started a two-week effort to contact Bishop Bonner, but it concluded with no success. Suddenly, I was led to contact a friend of many, many years, Bishop Melvin Williams, Jr. in Richmond, Virginia. He had introduced me to Bishop Ronald Carter during one of my visits there when Bishop Carter was conducting a revival. I was also made aware that Bishop Carter was then Chairman of the Board of Bishops for COOLJC. (That position is now held by Bishop Herbert Edwards from Greenville, South Carolina). After explaining my desire, Bishop Carter offered to intercede on my behalf. Now keep in mind that Sister Ruby Lloyd and I had tried to reach Bishop Bonner for two weeks. Fifteen minutes after hanging up with Bishop Carter, I received a call from Bishop Bonner. Upon sharing my reasons for wanting to reach him, he asked me, "Bishop, do I know you?" To which I replied, "Bishop Bonner, I have met you at several places where you were preaching, but no, you do not really know me." He then said, "Let me pray about it."

About a week later, an express letter arrived at Mt. Sinai Church, here in Martinsville. Upon seeing that the correspondence was from Bishop W. L. Bonner, there was nothing but joy, joy, joy... until I read the letter. In the communication, he was very congratulatory on my succeeding my father; but stated that he would be unable to come and minister for us. According to my wonderful wife "Glo," she had never seen me that down before. Being convinced that I had been led of the Lord to call Bishop

Bonner, his response was inexplicable. Yet, I did not feel released by the Spirit to call anyone else. So, what was I supposed to do?

What followed next was nothing short of Divine intervention. You see we wanted Bishop Bonner to minister in the ACCG Convocation the first Saturday in August 1995. As it turned out, he was scheduled to be in the Martinsville area the last Saturday in July 1995 to dedicate the new Fellowship Church, which is pastored by my brother and great friend, Bishop Phillip Calloway. The Spirit spoke to me and said, "Go to that service." When Bishop Bonner walked into the pulpit and greeted each minister (as he had done twenty years earlier), 1 said, "Praise the Lord, Bishop. I am J. C. Richardson, Jr. and praying that you will come back next Saturday to preach for us in Martinsville." Bishop Bonner shook my hand, smiled, and said, "Pastor, keep believing in miracles," and then went to his seat.

About twenty minutes into the sermon, Bishop Bonner said, "I am not going to finish this sermon tonight. But I tell you what I am going to do. I am coming back next Saturday to preach for that young man right there," and pointed at me. (My seat was to the far left of Bishop in the pulpit). You know, I went off rejoicing and thanking the Lord. A colleague of mine said to me later, "**Richardson, I am not sure if I ever heard you** speak in tongues before, but I heard you loud and clear tonight." Once I sobered up, I quickly and quietly sat down. After all, that night belonged to Bishop Calloway and the Fellowship Church. How dare I let my actions diminish the celebratory atmosphere of the occasion.

A week later, Pastor came to the Mt. Sinai Church for the first time to minister. And it was for the ACCG Holy Convocation in the consecration and installation worship for Bishop Betts, Bishop Lowery, and me. Three things happened that day that still stand out in my mind vividly, twelve years later. First, it was amazing how many people said that the voice, laughter, and mannerisms of Bishop Bonner reminded them of Bishop J. C. Richardson, Sr. Secondly, even though we had a gratuity prepared for him, he declined it, and has never taken any financial remuneration in the twelve years that he has come to Mt. Sinai and/or The Apostle Church of Christ in God. Thirdly, Bishop preached powerfully from the book of Joshua Chapter one, "As I was with Moses, so shall I be with you, Joshua." Oh, how the Spirit ministered to me through His servant, and I felt very ready for the challenge that awaited.

The 1995 International Convocation of COOLJC was held in Greensboro, NC which is only an hour's drive south of Martinsville; convening two weeks after the ACCG Convocation. That was also the year that Bishop Bonner retired as the presiding apostle and assumed the office of chief apostle. Further, it was during that convention that he invited me to come on board as a faculty member of the W. L. Bonner College. However, because of commitments with another institution then (Danville, Virginia Community College), I was unable to start until September 1997. Thus, at the writing of this book, I have just concluded my tenth year serving that special institution. And what a joy and privilege it has been.

In August 2005, my wife and I attended the COOLJC Convention in Columbia, SC. On that Friday morning, after it had officially closed, Pastor Bonner invited Lady Glo and me to meet him at the Lawson Library at W. L. Bonner College. During that time of sharing, I expressed my desire to write a book about him, and he readily acquiesced to my request. After which, I mentioned the title that had already been given to me: *A Man Like This.*

Being the son and the son-in-law of ministers (Bishop Robert L. Hairston is my late father-in-law), and having been in ministry over 35 years, it has been my opportunity to interact with many colleagues. In fact, my ministerial experiences have taken me places in most major Christian denominations including: Apostolics, Baptists (Primitive, Missionary, Full Gospel), Christians (Disciples of Christ), Methodist (African Methodist Episcopal, African Methodist Episcopal Zion, Christian Methodist Episcopal, and United Methodist), Lutherans, Presbyterians, Roman Catholics, Holiness, Pentecostals, Charismatics,

Nondenominational, Unitarian-Universalist, and even Muslim groups. And in all of these opportunities, I have never met a minister quite like Bishop William Lee Bonner. His is truly a rare uniqueness, the extremely high intellect he possesses coupled with a most unusual anointing sets him apart. Some may approach his level of intelligence while falling woefully short of his spirituality. Others may approach his level of anointing while falling way short of his intelligence level. In my opinion, Pastor Bonner appears to possess a genius I.Q., while also maintaining a "genius" level of spirituality. He is indeed a humble and remarkable servant of God, who is fully committed to doing the Lord's will at all cost.

My prayer and hope are that you will be as blessed by reading this book as I was writing it.

Chapter Two
From the Plantation in Georgia to the Pulpit in New York

Bishop William L. Bonner will be 86 years old on November 12, 2007, yet we do not see any noticeable difference in energy, stamina, or endurance in this man. He seems to just get better with age. And while many would be content to rest upon their laurels Pastor Bonner continues to be creative and innovative in his ministries.

In the past month (May 2007) I received two letters from the ministries of Pastor Bonner. One correspondence was inviting me to the newly renovated Refuge Temple in Columbia, South Carolina. The second was informing me of another proposed project; the acquisition of additional acres of land expanding the Columbia Complex to include a hotel, shopping center, and single-family homes. Currently, the ministry includes Refuge Temple, the Family Life Center, the W. L. Bonner College, retirement units, and living quarters for the college students. And even while all this activity is taking place in South Carolina, this is by no means the extent of the ministry of Pastor Bonner. To get a comprehensive look at him, one must also go to New York City, Detroit, Jackson, and Washington, DC, also where he serves as pastor.

Pastor Bonner was born into the farming family of Emmet and Janie Bonner in Georgia. And, according to him, he knew very, very early that farming was not his "cup of tea." Thus, the young man named William Lee quickly concluded that for him, the alternative to walking behind a mule was the "bright lights and big city". Part of the agenda that this young man had in mind was to make a lot of money. His aptitude for learning quickly enabled him to readily master many skills in the workforce, including brick masonry. He also discovered that he was blessed to build naturally. Construction, however, was not the only agenda item that God had for him. There was going to be an international spiritual building as well.

After aligning himself with the Refuge Temple in Harlem, New York, under the pastorate of Bishop R. C. Lawson, Bonner started his divinely ordained ascent in Kingdom building. Once his initial training had been done at the mother church, and then on Green Avenue in Brooklyn, New York, Bishop Lawson dispatched the young Elder Bonner to Detroit.

As many know, his efforts in the Motor City have really been blessed. Thousands of souls have come to the Lord through the ministry of Solomon's Temple. Like his other pastorates, Solomon's Temple has a holistic approach to ministering. It consists of the Family and Cultural Center, Library of Pentecostal History, and the Royal Palace Mall. All of this is in addition to the very successful media ministry, and a simply beautiful edifice.

As Solomon's Temple was evolving, the mother church in New York went through a major change in 1961 with the passing of Bishop Lawson. He was the founding pastor of Refuge and the establishmentarian of the Church of Om Lord Jesus Christ. Chief Apostle Lawson was also a voracious reader, song writer, anointed teacher, eloquent preacher, and gifted administrator. He was simply legendary. And while I never personally met him, I heard so many absolutely wonderful things about him from my father and other preachers. As a teenager, I do recall with vivid clarity, the passing of Bishop Lawson.

Living in Martinsville at that time, I was far removed by age and distance from the inner workings of Refuge and COOLJC during that critical period in Apostolic Church History. Yet, I recall Dad talking about what might possibly happen regarding the leadership of COOLJC. He had been a personal friend of Bishop H. J. Spencer, who was one of the senior bishops at that time. In fact, Bishop Spencer had conducted revivals at our church in Martinsville, and on a historical note, our current chairman of deacons, Nathaniel W. Carter, Sr. got saved and filled with the Holy Ghost in the 1950s during a revival conducted by Bishop Spencer.

Some people in om area speculated that either Bishop Spencer or Bishop John Purnell from Richmond might succeed Bishop Lawson. Those same people felt that the whole issue would have been moot had Bishop Smallwood Williams still been a part of COOLJC. His departure four years earlier (in 1957), had created a schism that was rather considerable. As I discovered later, the opinions regarding Bishop Williams succeeding Bishop Lawson were not just in our area. Many in and out of COOLJC were convinced that only his leaving the Organization prevented his becoming the second presiding apostle.

In an effort to fill in some of the historical gaps, I conducted an interview with Bishop Bonner at the W. L. Bonner College in March 2007. Having been an integral part of that time period, he shared accurate information regarding the sequence of events. Note his comments:

> I declined the presider's seat to avoid a split. (Bishop) H. J. Spencer (from Columbus, OH) became the second presider.

Continuing his remarks, Pastor further stated:

Not only did (Bishop) Spencer want the presider's (position) he also wanted to pastor the mother church. But they (Refuge in New York) had said that they wanted me as pastor. Bishop Spencer held it against me that I would not step aside for him to pastor Refuge.

The question was posed as to what happened next? The Bishop added these words:

> Bishop Spencer started a campaign to destroy me. And it went on for a number of years. Finally, at a meeting in Pittsburgh (Pennsylvania), I got fed up.

After spending some time in prayer to get direction as to how he should handle this very personal and extremely sensitive situation, he was led to do the following:

> I talked with Bishop Spencer and said if you do not stop what you are doing, which he knew was wrong, the Lord will put a curse on you. And if you do not change, it will happen, and you will not recover.

Apparently, Bishop Spencer did not believe or accept what the younger minister was saying because he would not recant his remarks to Pastor Bonner privately or in front of the other ministers. So, what happened next?

Before leaving Pittsburgh, Bishop Spencer had a stroke from which he never recovered. After the Lord showed Bishop Spencer that he was getting ready to come home, he sent for Pastor. In that conversation, Spencer asked Bonner to forgive him, after which the two men prayed together. Now that they were reconciled, Bishop Spencer was ready to make his departure, and shortly thereafter, he passed; thus, ending the era of the second presiding apostle of the Church of Our Lord Jesus Christ.

It was then that I asked Pastor Bonner, "Is that what started the kind of prayer life that you have now?" He responded that:

> My prayer life had its beginning in Solomon's Temple. It started in part as a reaction to my wife, Mother Bonner. She wanted to divorce me. When I asked why, she said that I should accept women preachers. I refused. She then said I will break you. She then moved out. And I had to pray to keep my sanity because I was in love with my wife with all my heart.

What one notices when talking with Pastor Bonner is this: Yes, he is and has been a very blessed man. At the same time, he has experienced some profoundly deep hurts in his life.

Shortly after the experience with Mother Bonner at home, the Bishop went to Africa to evaluate the status of the COOLJC churches there. What he discovered was a rather putrid situation. Mud huts were being used as churches. Centering his efforts in Bokeytown and Monrovia, the then presiding apostle started working diligently.

What started as a domestic problem in Detroit between a husband and wife now took on international implications. Based on information that had been shared with him by Mother Bonner, the president of Liberia told Bishop Bonner to leave Africa. This despite the fact that elementary and high schools, as well as a clinic, were all being erected. The day the Liberian Government was to take over the schools, a coup occurred killing the president who had sought the ouster of Pastor Bonner. That former president was replaced by a man named Sergent Doe, who restored everything that the Church of Our Lord Jesus Christ had. Added to the clinic and schools, the Bishop led the people in building Refuge Temple in Liberia, which has a seating capacity of twelve hundred people with a horseshoe balcony.

At this point he resumed talking about his prayer life, stating that these various experiences really solidified and emphasized the importance of daily and consistent prayer.

> When I pray, it is not just asking, but it is thanking Him for being good to me. That (also) leads into praying for (other) people. I read their requests and lay before the Lord. People know that God will answer them if they get to Pastor Bonner.

Elucidating more regarding prayer, he added:

> I enjoy talking to the King of Kings and the Lord of Lords because He talks back. (Further), I discovered that I can control and defeat principalities and powers.

Looking at where Dr. Bonner is now, one tends to think he has always been here in terms of his spiritual development. But notice what happened to him before he fully understood the power of prayer.

> There was a period in my life I was so depressed that I wanted to die. One day I had gone to the 22nd floor of a bank building to discuss some business. But while waiting (on his appointment), Satan told me to just jump out of the window. They had floor to ceiling windows. Satan said if you jump, everything would be over, and you would have no more problems. Thank God, I had the strength to resist what the enemy had brought to me.

It is very important when we write about a giant prayer warrior to recognize that he has not always been a giant. There have been so many obstacles in the face of those who have grown to be the kind of living examples for Christ that we seek to emulate. How true these words are when applied to Pastor Bonner.

Chapter Three
The Apostolic Dilemma

In an attempt to look critically at the life of Bishop William Lee Bonner, some attention has to be given to his writings. In them, we discover something noteworthy about this humble servant. As much as he is a creative visionary; and he really is, there is still an amazing consistency regarding his scriptural understanding and biblical teachings. On the one hand, he seems to be ever evolving, and yet he maintains a very rigorous, if not rigid stance in the traditional Apostolic doctrines.

So, let us look first at the books titled *The Apostolic Dilemma* and *The Apostolic Dilemma Volume Two Women's Liberation.* In the former treatise, Pastor Bonner addresses the issue of gay men and lesbian women; the homosexual life style. While in the latter work, focus is on the biblical role of women in the church. These two subjects have certainly been at the root of much discussion in the Christian Church in recent years. Some religious leaders have even changed their long-held positions on them. Let's see though what changes Pastor Bonner has made.

It was in the fall of 1975 when the bishop delivered a series of lectures on homosexuality at the Church of Christ Bible Institute (CCBI) in New York City. Bishop R. C.

Lawson founded this religious educational center many years ago.

Quoting from Dr. Bonner's book:

A dilemma is a situation requiring a choice between equally objectionable alternatives... a problem that cannot be satisfactorily resolved.[1]

Pastor Bonner continues with the following remarks:

The dilemma arises when people try to solve their problems without the help and guidance of God.

... The Bible, in speaking of this problem reveals important facts at which we should take a good look. One of these facts is that homosexuality has plagued the human race for many millenniums. It isn't a new phenomenon.[2]

Directing the reader to a scriptural passage, Pastor Bonner selects verses that give attention to the biblical character Lot, as he dealt with this issue.

---

[1] William L. Bonner, The Apostolic Dilemma, New York, s.n., 1976, p. 3.
[2] Ibid., pp. 3-4

> Way back in the days of Lot, the practice of homosexuality was widespread... When two angels... appearing as men, visited Lot thinking they were new men in town, the men of Sodom wanted to have sexual relations with them.[3]

Note the scripture that is used to reference this episode.

> the men of the city even the men of Sodom, compassed the house round, both old and young, all the people from every quarter: And they called unto Lot, and said unto him, where are the men which came in to thee this night? Bring them out unto us, that we may know them. And Lot... said, I pray you brethren, do not so wickedly." (Genesis 19:4-7)

According to biblical research, the Hebrew verb for know is generally used for normal sexual relations between a male and female (Genesis 4:1). Here though know is being used to describe the "perversion" of homosexual acts between men.

---

[3] Ibid., p. 4.

Pastor Bonner goes on to share with us:

> It is important to understand that sexual desires are inborn. God made men and women for each other...

The power of the mind in thought and imagination can create almost any given situation when there is expressed desire within to do it. The mind of the person becomes a research center discovering ways to express the emotions or sexual desires. During the ages from twelve to twenty and sometimes younger, many young people get into difficulties because they didn't understand how to deal with their emotions with their passionate desires and eager imaginations, they create means of expression, right or wrong, normal or abnormal." These words are also from his book.

> The passions and the will to express them at this young age are explosive forces that should be dealt with positively by parents, the church, and organizations dealing with youth.[4]

Writing like this in the 1970s by a traditional Black Apostolic pastor was on a level that was considered pioneering. While many would be quick to condemn

---
[4] Ibid., p. 5.

homosexuality as wrong, not nearly as many would spend the effort to address it.

The enormity and complexity of this issue require more than "if you are homosexual, you are going to hell." That solicits a lot of "amens" and may even stroke the ego of the proclaiming preacher. However, does it really speak to young people in their late teens or early twenties who are seriously wrestling with this issue?

While continuing refer to Scriptures that condemn the gay lifestyle, Pastor Bonner presents the need for the church and family to address the problem boldly and consciously. Note the following:

> If a man also lie with mankind, as he lieth with a woman, both of them have committed an abomination: they shall surely be put to death. (Lev 20: 13)

In this scripture, note the word "abomination." A part of its definition is that which is detestable to God; that which is odious, despised, hated, filthy, or stinking rotten. It would appear then that homosexuality in this context is among the sins that are very distasteful and repugnant to the Lord.

Now listen to these additional words that Pastor Bonner presents on the subject:

> Homosexuality is a sickness that creeps upon the individual through experimentation... They (young people) have these strong desires and... don't know how to channel them (properly)... Experimentation through masturbation is usually the first means of sexual expression
>
> The frequency of... masturbation in high school age young people is great. If young men experiment together with their bodies... this can be one of the ways they become homosexuals. And the same goes for young women.[5]

Showing that he has given serious and prayerful thought to this subject Dr. Bonner leads us further into the discourse. In his book, *The Apostolic Dilemma*, he titled Chapter V, "The Homosexual, A Fugitive From Women." There are several points that need to be shared with you. (Of course, I strongly recommend your reading the entire book.) First, Pastor contends that one reason the (male) homosexual runs from women is because he finds loving relationships with women to be most painful and very unsatisfying. He seems to be thoroughly unable to show

---

[5] Ibid., p. 7.

any kind of sexual expression toward a woman. Therefore, he turns to other men.

This theory as Pastor Bonner calls it, of the homosexual being a fugitive from women is really based on their fears and lack of confidence as men. What comes into the equation now is the psychological state, or well-being of that particular person. Essentially, there would appear to be very deep-seated emotional issues. And as painful as it may be, that person needs to really wrestle with and address these concerns, comprehensively and prayerfully.

While Pastor Bonner does not exclude the adverse impact of the environment or other mitigating circumstances, he readily concedes that one must of necessity do some psychoanalysis. Or to put it another way, he says:

> When a man runs from a woman, a soft, beautiful, sweet and darling creature, he has to have deep seated psychological problems.[6]

Secondly, Pastor has an attention-grabbing concept about single sex education versus co-education that is quite intriguing. He puts it like this.

---

[6] Ibid., p. 25.

> I seriously question the value of an all-girls, or all boys school. Co-educational training is a healthier environment. Creating separate schools for boys and girls leads to the development of an unhealthy psychological environment.[7]

Because that was originally stated in his writings in 1975, you know there was a question. That was, if he still felt the same way about same sex education as opposed to co-educational opportunities. His response was in the affirmative. There has been no change in his viewpoint on the subject. One of Pastor's points is that single sex education, especially during the formative years, keeps the child from cultivating normal male-female relationships.

Thirdly, homosexuality in the church contributes to another problem. Most local congregations are dominated by females. In fact, it is not unusual for a parish to have two to four females for every male member. So, when single saved women desire to marry a spouse who is also saved, that is often very difficult.

This reminds me of an interim pastorate that I once held in another state. One Sunday afternoon, an informal discussion with several of the single sisters turned to the subject of matrimony. As their shepherd, I was asked to get serious about praying for saved prospective husbands to come their way. Since I really did not know a lot about that

---

[7] Ibid., p. 29.

particular city, several questions were raised, about the availability of males in the area. And I shall never forget their response.

> Pastor, when you take away the married men, drug addicts, men in prison, and homosexuals, there is really no one else left from which to choose.

That was told to me well over twenty years ago in my ministry, and it does not appear that much has changed in that regard in 2007.

Pastor Bonner speaks of other concerns relative to male homosexuality in this way:

> Many young virgins continue to be so throughout their lifetime because of the scarcity of quality men around to marry. They refuse to accept just any man for physical and sexual satisfaction. Rather than do this, they dedicate their lives to God... such a woman should be praised because she hasn't chosen an easy life... Men are not faced with this problem because of the abundance of dedicated women in the church... Realizing this condition... many women to choose from, it is puzzling as to why we have so many fugitives from women. Homosexuality is not a curse

put on man by God. This is the curse man brings on himself because he goes after strange flesh and rejects the Word of God.[8]

In the same way that gay men are fugitives from women, lesbians can be viewed as fugitives from men. Looking at the position put forth by the Bishop, lesbianism must be addressed with the same type of committed, prayerful attention as gay men. The need for greater focus on the issue is due in part to the greater efforts of the gay community and their supporters to present it as an acceptable lifestyle.

In 1975 Pastor felt that this was a priority issue that the church must address. However, with the consecration of an openly gay person to the bishopric, V. Gene Robinson, is the church now considering this issue differently? Does Bishop Robinson's elevation in the American Episcopal Church signal a new and more open view by the religious community? But another view is a part of the dialogue. Some believe efforts to make homosexuality acceptable is simply a part of the movement toward apostasy before the return of our Lord, Jesus Christ.

What is certain though is this. In one-way or another, the church has to take a stand with a plausible explanation

---

[8] Ibid., p. 29.

supporting that position. In taking his stand, note what Pastor says:

> We can ask the same question concerning women as we did... men. What makes a woman flee from seeking sexual satisfaction with a man and seek it with another woman?... Experimentation and masturbation in their youth, plus disappointment in some earlier love relationship with a man, or possibly, disgust with men... (even) their fathers turned them off from men.[9]

While reading this book by Bishop Bonner, I kept reflecting on what we as clergy should do to be more effective in various areas of ministry. As my father told me when he pondered retiring from the pastorate in 1991, "Times have changed since I first went into the ministry and some things are very different." The higher visibility of homosexuality is one of those changes. There seems to be reluctance on the part of some in the clergy, to address certain issues because of the discomfort level. The gay community is very real and is becoming much more savvy and sophisticated in presenting its agenda. One tactic seems to be using well-known people within various ethnic groups to publicly endorse the gay lifestyle. These persons usually have what we call "celebrity status". This tactic is

---

[9] Ibid., p. 33.

used to openly validate what is typically taboo or unacceptable.

Perhaps, there is a need for us in the clergy to evaluate what is currently being done in our respective localities. One way is to find out literature and services agencies provide. You do not have to agree with them, but you must be informed in order to make intelligent and helpful decisions.

The "head in the sand" strategy long ago ceased being a viable approach. That is what we have done with some other issues like marriage and divorce, for instance. How many pastors have serious pre-marital counseling sessions before conducting weddings? If we are opposed to divorce, don't we have an equally important responsibility to provide leadership and direction that will help determine couples' readiness for marriage? With far too many in the clergy, if two people announce their intent to get married, that is the only prerequisite for many of us to then perform the ceremony. Many times, prayer and pre-marital counseling can help to alert the minister about the level of readiness a couple has for marriage. The clergy must be much more proactive in some matters rather than reactive.

I recall a counseling session with a person who was separating because of the physical violence she had endured in her marriage. Yes, they were both "saved" and very active church members. Rather than leave though, her pastor counseled her to just go in another room and lock the door. Wouldn't you know that the husband had keys to every room in the house that the wife had. Amazing!!! While pre-marital counseling may not have revealed that particular issue, it is likely that some tendencies or concerns may have surfaced, that would have certainly raised very pertinent questions.

It seems to me that the Bishop has laid out the need for us to consider a feasible paradigm that will enable a pastor and local assembly to minister effectively to those in the gay community. In our congregations there just may be a person like the young lady that he talks about in his book, *The Apostolic Dilemma:*

> I've had these tendencies ever since I can remember. In high school, I' d look at this or that girl and I'd have the desire... to know her better. I didn't just want her. I'd want her to want me... I don't like having sex with a guy... I never enjoyed it (with a male). I never had an orgasm with a guy.[10]

By now, you should have concluded that based on Pastor Bonner's understanding of the scriptures, the homosexual lifestyle is categorically wrong; further, it is also sinful. But he raises a challenge for us to minister in

---

[10] Ibid., p. 35

ways that will lead all of God's people to Christ for healing and salvation.

In developing his position Pastor listed a number of scriptures that I would like to share with you. These references are from the King James version unless otherwise stated. Genesis 2:18, 21-24

> And the Lord God said, It is not good that man should be alone, I will make him a help meet for him.

> And the Lord God caused a deep sleep to fall upon Adam, and he slept: and he took one of his ribs, and closed up the flesh instead thereof;

> And the rib which the Lord God had taken from man, made he a woman and brought her unto man.

> And Adam said, this is now bone of my bones, and flesh of my flesh: she shall be called Woman because she was taken out of Man.

> Therefore, shall a man leave his father and his mother, and shall cleave unto his wife: and they shall be one flesh.

One thing that we come to understand in this passage is the importance of the marital relationship to our Lord. And that relationship has _always_ between a man and a woman. Remember, it was God who said, "It is not good that man should be alone." Thus, God commanded that a man shall cleave to his wife. This set the divine pattern for what marriage is supposed to be. Nowhere does it say in scripture that marriage is to be between people of the same gender. Genesis 4:1

> And Adam knew Eve his wife; and she conceived, and bore Cain, and said, Lord I have gotten a man from the Lord.

The word knew (or to know) in such a context refers to having sexual relations within the confines of a marriage between a man and a woman (husband and wife).

> But before they lay down, the men of the city even the men of Sodom, compassed the house round, both old and young, all the people from every quarter.

> And they called unto Lot and said unto him, where are the men which came into thee this night? Bring them out unto us that we may _know_ them.

> And Lot went out at the door unto them, and shut the door after him, And said, I pray you brethren, do not so wickedly. Genesis 19:4-7

Several sources of research point to these men in Sodom wanting to engage in homosexual acts with the visitors of Lot. Just as important was the repeated efforts by Lot to keep these acts from taking place. It was all very clear to Lot that he, under no circumstances, would be a part of these homosexual proclivities being carried out toward his guests. Leviticus 20: 13 (New King James Version)

> If a man lies with a male as he lies with a woman, both of them have committed an abomination. They shall surely be put to death. Their blood shall be upon them.

Now, according to the Law of Moses, anyone found guilty of adultery, bestiality, or sodomy (homosexual acts), that person could be put to death. Obviously, the belief was that each of these sins was so egregious as to warrant termination of life of the transgressor. It also suggests that specific sins by heterosexuals have the same weight of severity as those by homosexuals. That would certainly eliminate excuses and self-made justifications that straight people use to rationalize certain activities while condemning those in the gay community:

> For this cause God gave them up unto vile affections: for even their women did change that natural use into that which is against nature: And likewise, also the men leaving the natural use of the woman, burned in their lust one toward another; men with men working that which is unseemly and receiving in themselves that recompense of their error which was meet. And even as they did not like to retain God in their knowledge, God gave them over to a reprobate mind to those things which are not convenient (or fitting).
> Romans 1:26-28

Growing up in the Black Apostolic Church, there were selective words in scripture that just had an awesome impact whenever they were used. One such word is reprobate. Sermons and Bible lessons heard in my youth can be recalled along with a profound sense of apprehension at hearing one of those "dreaded" words.

Reprobate means that which is depraved or without morals. Another definition also includes that which is debased. In my youth, we came to believe if one ever became a reprobate, that person was way beyond spiritual redemption. For it indicated that he/she had willfully, intentionally, and repeatedly committed acts, with forethought that were contrary to the Will and Word of God.

Such a person was believed to be dangerous and even harmful to the church folk.

It is therefore in the context of spiritual decay that sins including homosexuality are referred to in the scriptural passage in Romans 1:26-28. According to one source:

> Homosexuality is sin. In this passage (Romans 1:27) the point is not that homosexuality is a sin that should be punished. Rather homosexuality itself is the punishment. Having rejected God and became idolaters, some men have been given over to their shameful passions. Thus, they receive in themselves the penalty of their error.[11]

My understanding of the position of Bishop Bonner is that at no point can the church say yes to homosexuality as an acceptable lifestyle. And his viewpoint is of such because the Holy Word does not validate that lifestyle as pleasing or acceptable to our Lord.

---

[11] King James Study Bible, Nashville, TN: Thomas Nelson Publishers, p. 1880.

Chapter Four
Women, Ministry, and the Church

In the 1970's, the Women's Liberation Movement caught fire and spread throughout the United States of America. Many long-held traditions, some even sacred, were seriously challenged. The result led to some historic and monumental changes in American society. What were the defined roles of women before the movement versus since the movement? What was posed over and over was how should these questions be addressed in the church versus non-church areas.

To better grasp the thinking and teaching of Pastor Bonner on this subject, let us look at his religious history. Bishop Lawson was the spiritual father of Bishop Bonner. And part of the reason for the COOLJC coming into existence was the issue of women in ministry. It was in 1919, the young Elder Lawson resigned his pastorate in Columbus, OH, from a congregation that was an affiliate of the Pentecostal Assemblies of the World (PAW).

For a good while even then, PAW had women ministers, some of whom were also pastors. Dr. Lawson concluded that ordained female clergy was contrary to scripture. He also reached a determination that divorce and remarriage in the church were also contrary to scriptural teachings. So, these two issues were of paramount importance to Bishop Lawson. His subsequent divinely led trek went from Columbus to New York City, where the Church Of Our Lord Jesus Christ was birthed in the "Cradle of Refuge."

These two issues continue to be very important doctrinal teachings in COOLJC. It was thus in this kind of setting that Dr. Bonner experienced spiritual rebirth. Added to the excellent teaching that he received from Bishop Lawson, he also spent major qualitative time praying and studying God's word for himself.

From his prayer ministry grew a need to put some of his concerns in writing. Two of the books he penned are titled, The Apostolic Dilemma, Volume Two, Women's Liberation and Three Women, Sarah, Rebecca, Jezebel. These publications adequately capture the viewpoint that Pastor Bonner has developed relative to his perceived role of women in scriptures.

One of the more fascinating aspects about him is his consistency over a number of years; decades in fact. Apostolic Dilemma, Volume Two was written in 1976, while Three Women was published in 1993. One is struck by his similarity of thought over an almost twenty-year time period. So, with these books as our foundational basis, let us then examine his teaching on the role of women in the church.

According to Bishop, "One reason for its (The Women's Liberation) divisiveness is that the church has not dealt with it from a biblical point of view, but has largely followed the trend and fashion of the world."[12]

In looking at that statement, one is reminded of Old Testament Israel during the time of Samuel, the priest and judge. Once Samuel was advanced in age nearing retirement, the people were adamant about not having the sons of Samuel succeed him because they were rascals. As right as the people were in not wanting the sons of Samuel, they were equally wrong in not seeking the Lord for direction. Rather, they said, "Give us a king like other nations." There should always be a resounding concern when leaders in the church seek to emulate worldly trends. Generally, their impact on the church is profoundly negative. It is the church that is supposed to influence the world not the other way around.

As he elucidates on this issue, the Chief Apostle uses I Corinthians, chapter 12, as a contextual departure. This passage uses the human body parabolically to enumerate the parts of the Body of Christ.

> The pastor is the head of the local church assembly as God's under-shepherd. He is not the head of the body of Christ... In using the human body, the Apostle Paul gives us a spiritual revelation. The various parts of the body have assigned places and functions to them by

---

[12] William L. Bonner, The Apostolic Dilemma Volume Two: Women's Liberation. New York: 1976, p.1.

God... Then what part of the body and function is the woman? What part of the body is the man?[13]

Some believe that Paul was expressing both the unity and diversity of the body of Christ. This can also be applied to the local assembly in a spiritual context. And for any local assembly to function in the Lord's will all members need to know their role and work in harmony,

Reading his book further, Pastor Bonner informs us that the confusion over the woman's role in the church comes often from a misunderstanding of the following scripture in Galatians 3:27-28:

> For as many of you as have been baptized into Christ have put on Christ. There is neither Jew nor Greek, there is neither bond nor free, there is neither male nor female, for ye all are in Christ Jesus.

It is quite obvious from the context, he says, that the Apostle is dealing with the subject of salvation. On this matter, God makes absolutely no distinction between male and female. Just like a person's race, culture, pedigree, or ethnicity, one's gender is never a barrier to salvation. So then if the problem is not in gender as regards to salvation, when, or where does this confusion arise? One can see a

---

[13] Ibid., p 3.

rather definitive response to that question in these words by the Bishop:

> Men and women have by the Spirit been baptized into the body of Christ and are equally saved. But when it comes to how the two sexes function in the church, God makes a distinction. The head of the woman is man (I Corinthians 11 :3). I permit not a woman to teach or usurp authority over a man. (I Timothy 2:12).[14]

Giving further enlightenment regarding this particular biblical interpretation, we are informed that,

> Two truths about the woman are being discussed here. One deals with her salvation, and the other deals with her place in the divine order as it related to the man. The present attitude is that a woman can hold any office that a man can. But this is absolutely... contrary to the Word of God. By virtue of her subordinate role in the divine order, a woman is prevented from occupying any position of authority which places her over a man. And if she is a preacher, pastor, bishop, apostle... she is in a position of authority over

---

[14] Ibid., p. 4.

everyone in the congregation. Occupying such a position is out of the Will of God.[15]

As he continues to share insights about this very pertinent subject, Pastor looks at the natural body and spiritual body in similar ways. He says that the head is the controlling factor in the human body, or the body of Christ. In the head lies the control center, the brain. We are thusly taught that the pastor of the local assembly sets the spiritual temperature. He can determine if joy is expressed, if knowledge is propagated, or if something else takes place. Again though, the local assembly is different in one aspect from the total body of Christ, which is never weak. His teaching is that while the <u>Church</u> is overcoming and victorious, some local assemblies are like weak links in a chain. It is therefore the pastor who can either hinder or help his members. An example of the importance of this role is found in the book of Revelation 2:1-4. "Unto the angel of the Church of Ephesus write... thou hast left thy first love."

According to our Lord Jesus in St. John 13:35, "By this shall all men know that you are my disciples if you have love one for another." Love then is a primary fundamental ingredient of the Christ-like lifestyle. When a local Christian assembly does not display that attribute, then a very, very serious problem has developed. The role of the pastor in leading the flock to that awareness of love and

---

[15] Ibid., pp. 4-5.

implementation is critical. The local assembly does not need to be out of love and out of order. Both are important to Kingdom building as the Lord wills.

We are further instructed that:

Man had nothing to do with this arrangement. God has decided in an absolutely... clear manner precisely how the church is to function, who is at the head... and who has the subordinate position. Man, in his misunderstanding of the Word of God has permitted women to commit error. Many have ordained women to the ministry contrary to the Word of God.[16]

Bear in mind however that the divine order for church administration was mandated by the Lord. And "God (has) set the members in the body as it pleased him." (I Corinthians 12:18)

Please allow me to share with you other scriptures that are presented in *Apostolic Dilemma, Volume Two.* In it we are told that the key to our understanding God's divine order can be found in the book of Genesis. After Adam and Eve disobeyed the Lord by eating of the tree of knowledge of good and evil, there were consequences. There are always

---

[16] Ibid., p. 6.

consequences for any child of God who willfully and intentionally disobeys the Lord.

In the midst of blessings, one must still accept accountability for all acts of disobedience. An example of that in Scripture was King David. Even as God was preparing for His son Jesus to come through the line and lineage of David, which was, I believe, one awesome blessing, David had some burdens to carry, His whole episode and involvement with Bath-Sheba brought pain to the heart of God. While his anointing to the kingship had been divinely orchestrated, his disobedience created havoc for his relationship with the Lord. David's exploits with Bath-Sheba also factored into his inability to provide the type of fatherly leadership needed to address the situation between Prince Amnon and his half-sister, Tamar in II Samuel, chapter 13.

Quite frankly, it is very much questionable if Amnon would have had the nerve, or the audacity to demonstrate such lack of respect of raping Tamar, had he not known about the misdeeds of King David. When David willfully took advantage of Bath-Sheba, and plotted to have her husband, Uriah, killed, king or no king, respect for him had to diminish considerably in the eyes and hearts of so many.

When we go back to the book of Genesis, we can note several things.

Genesis 2:7 - "And the Lord God formed man of the dust of the ground and breathed into his nostrils the breath of life; and man became a living soul."

Genesis 2:15 - "And the Lord God took the man and put him into the Garden of Eden to dress it and to keep it."

Genesis 2: 19-23 (NKJV) - "Out of the ground the Lord God formed every beast of the field and every bird of the air and brought them to Adam to see what he would call them. And whatever Adam called each living creature, that was its name. So, Adam gave names to all cattle, to the birds of the air, and to every beast of the field. But for Adam, there was not a helper comparable to him. And the Lord God caused a deep sleep to fall on Adam and he slept; and He took one of his ribs and closed up the flesh in its place. Then the rib which the Lord God had taken from man, He made into a woman and He brought her to the man. And Adam said:

This is now bone of my bones and flesh of my flesh; she shall be called woman because she was taken out of man.

Now with the three preceding scriptures as our backdrop, there is a point to be made here. Those who support the position of women in a subordinate position in the church can see its initial application in Genesis. The Lord had maintained a rather extensive relationship with Adam prior to the appearance of Eve. As you fully know, even the command to stay away from the tree of knowledge of good and evil was given to Adam alone. Further, a thorough review of these passages seems to imply that man is indeed the head of woman in the divine order.

Once disobedience toward God's commands had been committed by Adam and Eve, they both received punishment from the Lord. However, executing that punishment, we now see a change in God's divine order of them. In fact, Scripture appears to reinforce their respective positions even after their fall. Look at Genesis 3:16 in two different scriptural versions.

> KJV "Unto the woman he said, I will greatly multiply thy sorrow and thy conception; in sorrow thou shalt bring forth children and thy desire shall be to thy husband, and he shall rule over thee."

> TEV "Then God said to the woman, 'you shall bear children in intense pain and suffering; yet even so, you shall welcome your husband's affections, and he shall be your master.

One of the reasons this scripture is such a good starting point is that from it, references are made to various passages in the New Testament. And those scriptures are lifted up to validate the specific and different roles of men and women in the church today.

One scripture to which Pastor Bonner invites our attention is I Corinthians, Chapter 11.

> vs. 3 - "But I would have you know that the head of every man is Christ; and the head of the woman is the man; and the head of Christ is God."

> vs. 7 - "For a man ought not to cover his head, forasmuch as he is the image and glory of God: but the woman is the glory of man."

> vs. 8 - "For the man is not of the woman; but the woman of the man."

> vs. 9 - "Neither was the man created for the woman, but the woman for the man."

Though some dismiss Paul here as abrasively chauvinistic and sexist, there is another view. The Apostle was addressing issues that had been established under the

Law. And Paul recognized or understood that some of these same issues had not been abrogated in Christ. If then the woman is no longer subordinated to the man in the divine order, then man is no longer subordinated to Christ, and neither is Christ to God. A Christian man is a part of the Holy Church body headed by Jesus Christ. It seems then that we have to accept all of this or none of this, in terms of the divine order in the Church.

Yes, it is emphatically true that Genesis 1:27 states, "So God created man in his image, in the image of God created he him; male and female created he them." But in I Corinthians. chapter 11, some believe that Paul used the word <u>image</u> in a restricted sense here. Man is uniquely in the image of God because he was given dominion over the earth. And this happened <u>before</u> the creation of woman. So then whatever dominion and/or authority woman has is delegated to her by her head - man. To augment the point Paul reminded the church at Corinth that woman was created after man for man. He does go on to say that men and women categorically need each other. But mutual need does not negate or change divinely defined positions.

In his exhaustive attention to this sometimes-contentious issue, Pastor focused on some other scriptures as well. Let me particularly direct you to I Corinthians 14:34.

> Let your women keep silent in the churches: for it is not permitted unto them to speak, but they are

commanded to be under obedience, as also saith the law.

Interpreting or exegeting this verse, Pastor Bonner has these words to share:

> The law already settled the question on women's conduct in public, and Paul says by the inspiration of God that this fact applies to women in the Church Age also. Remember we talked about rightly dividing The Word... Well, some Old Testament scriptures still apply today. Women are not to engage doctrinal disputes, points of order, or any public church business in a manner which violates her subordinate role to man. If she does... She is... ignoring her head.[17]

In the words of W.L. Bonner, women should not do anything to usurp the man's position of leadership. Turn your attention now to the book of Ephesians, chapter 5, verses 22-25, where these words are recorded (modem translation).

> You wives must submit to your husband's leadership In the same way you submit to the Lord. For a husband is in charge of his wife in the same way Christ is in charge of his body, the church. He gave his very life to

---

[17] Ibid. p. 9.

take care of it and be its Saviour! So, wives must willingly obey your husbands in everything, just as the church obeys Christ. And you husbands show the same kind of love to your wives as Christ showed to the church who died for her to make her holy and clean washed by baptism and God's Word.

On several occasions, while teaching married couples, I have often asked, what is the basis or foundation for this passage of scripture? In most cases, the men respond, "obedience." But the women always respond that "love" is the foundation for this scriptural passage. That is mentioned because, I believe, a lot of men misinterpret those verses. Anytime I asked the women, "Would you have a problem following the leadership of a man (your man) if you knew without a doubt that he was willing to die for you like Christ died for the church?" The response is always resounding in support of such men. Love and obedience are some key words in this passage.

And, men cannot condemn or expect women to follow their leadership obediently, if they are not consistently expressing to her agape love. The love from the men is really what enables the women to function in a subordinated role. When this love is put into action then this:

Love will not allow men to disrespect women.

Love will not allow men to abuse women.

Love will not allow men to treat women like children.

Even worse, love will not allow men to treat women like property or objects.

Early in our marriage, my wife helped me to quickly process and solve a problem. Each of our then small children came to me for some money. I asked the children, "What do you need it for?" And they answered me. Since I was satisfied that the reasons were sufficient, their daddy complied with the requests for funds.

A little later my wife came to me and said she needed some money; to which I responded "for what?" Her response to me was "Just forget it." It quickly became obvious to me that my response to her was as if she were my child, and not my spouse. We then decided that a petty cash fund would be available to either of us as needed once primary bills were paid. And neither of us owed the other an explanation, nor needed the other's permission to use those funds from petty cash. That approach has continued to work well for my wife, Glo, and me. And, we just recently celebrated forty-five years of courtship and marriage.

If we are Spirit filled Christians, it would appear too inconsistent for men to treat women void of dignity, love, and respect. The Scriptures remind us that Christ is our example. And when has He disrespected His Church?

Let us now look at the teaching of Pastor on some aspects of the role of women in the Church. People often talk about what is called the Five-Fold Ministry. One place this is found is in Ephesians 4: 11. These include apostles, prophets, evangelists, pastors, and teachers. In his book, there is attention given to the ministry of prophecy or the prophetess. He fully acknowledges that women were most certainly used in that capacity by the Lord.

In his words, two women in the New Testament who did the "work" of a prophetess never had the title. They were Elizabeth the mother of John the Baptist, and Mary the mother of our Lord. Using his definition of prophecy, which is to foretell something, he goes to the book of Luke, chapter one, verses 39-48, 52. This passage of scripture is considered by some to have profoundly important implications, because of the events that followed.

Two points need to be mentioned right here. First in verse 43:

> But why is this granted to me that the mother of my Lord should come to me?

Elizabeth was speaking prophetically to Mary. For the Spirit had enabled Elizabeth to know and speak that Mary was indeed carrying a child who was to be our Lord. And then we note verse 48.

> For He has regarded the lowly state of His maidservant. For behold, henceforth all generations will call me blessed.

Just as the Spirit moved on Elizabeth to speak here, He caused Mary to utter words that speak to the honor that she now receives. Generations continue to marvel at the phenomenal blessing that was given to Mary to be the mother of our Lord. And, for Pastor, these two women each carried the title prophetess.

In addition to Elizabeth and Mary, we next focus on a very familiar personality in the Old Testament; Deborah in the book of Judges. While many who advocate for women in the ordained ministry, will use this judge as an Old Testament forerunner, Pastor looks at it in a different way. First Deborah was, in his mind, a prophetess. This position is supported by the passage in Judges 4:1-24 with special attention to verses 8, 9, and 21.

Essentially one named Barak, a military general, was expected to lead Israel's charge in battles. However Barak was not willing to go without the physical presence and support of Deborah, the Judge. And, while this woman of God indicated her intentions to go, she had a prophetic word for him.

> So, she said, 'I will surely go with you; nevertheless, there will be no glory for you in the journey you are taking for the Lord will sell Sisera into the hand of a woman. (verse 9)

Verse nine in Judges, chapter four, came to pass in verse 21.21. Jael, a woman, and not Barak, got the honor for killing Sisera. His lack of faith, his lack of courage, or something else prevented him from basking in the triumphant victory over the enemy.

The second title that is noteworthy for Deborah was Mother. This was given in Judges 5:6-7,

> In the days of Shamgar and of Joel the main roads were deserted. Travelers used the narrow, crooked side paths. Israel's population dwindled until Deborah became a mother to Israel.

In the teaching by the Bishop, because a woman has the ministry of prophecy does not mean that she has been called to the pastorate, or the ordained clergy. Some of what Deborah did was because the men were not willing to accept the responsibility that had been assigned to them. Secondly, her title as mother of Israel was not only an honor, it was more fitting with that traditionally assigned to woman in the divine order. His primary point though is this. The scriptures do not give to a woman a position in the Kingdom that will be out of order with what God mandated in the Old Testament and the New Testament.

Let's look at a gift that the Holy Spirit gives to men and women. This arose in the process of my interviewing Pastor Bonner regarding a personal experience while up in the Apostolic Church. Back in the day, my father invited this lady to minister at our church. We were told that she had the gift of impartation. That simply meant when she prayed for people laying on hands, those individuals received the baptism of the Holy Spirit, while speaking in tongues. And this lady was also a pastor. In my mind, there seemed to be divine justification for her to pastor since she had the gift of impartation. That was also the rationale of so many others who may have grown up in our tradition.

In response, Pastor Bonner spoke of a well-known missionary in the Detroit Church, Solomon's Temple. That lady, Mother Pandora Williams, had been used by God in a similar way for years. At no time though has she ever expressed a "calling" or a desire to enter the preaching ministry. Nor has she ever sought to move her membership to an assembly that will allow, if not encourage, her to pursue the ordained clergy. His point was, just because the Spirit chooses to use a woman in that ministry, does not mean that she is being prepared to pastor, or head a local congregation.

After reflecting on that response, some other concerns surfaced in my mind. Certain groups would almost insist that such a woman had to preach because that is obviously what "the Lord was saying to her." It does cause us to wonder at times how "getting the call to preach" is tied to a particular culture, denominational affiliation, or religious tradition. While it would be difficult to do, it is still worthwhile to consider primary uniformed standards of preparation before entering the Gospel Ministry. If the Old Testament prophets had schools, and if the Lord Jesus took three years to equip His Apostles, shouldn't the rest of us get some training?

It is also worth noting that persons with wonderful gifts in one area are so often pushed toward the clergy in the Apostolic Church. One of my closest and dearest friends is Deacon Richard King here at Mt. Sinai where we both grew up under the pastorate of Bishop J.C. Richardson, Sr. As teenagers, and in our early twenties, Richard was very interested in studying the Word of God, and spent countless hours in prayer, research, and sitting under the teaching of my father.

As Richard began to develop and evolve, not only did his knowledge of Scripture expand, but it became obvious that he was an enormously gifted teacher. Subsequently, many would share with him, "Brother, you have been called to preach." There was only one problem though; Deacon King never felt that "preaching" was his calling. Furthermore, each time he sought the direction from the Lord by fasting, praying, and talking with his pastor, he never concluded that the ordained ministry was his calling.

Had he listened to people and not to the voice of God, in all probability, Deacon King would be doing what he had not been called to do; and doing what would not be pleasing to his Lord.

Today, Mt. Sinai continues to be blessed by his informative and anointed teaching ministry. He, along with a staff of ministers, deacons, and missionaries assist the pastor in the teaching ministry of our church. My prayer is that others will not have to go through what Deacon King confronted. Folks need to back off from attempting to put people where they are not supposed to be. Just as Deacon King is most effective doing what he has been called and appointed to do, Pastor Bonner is suggesting that all seek to be more cognizant of divinely assigned roles and positions. That way, the workers will be ever so efficacious in Kingdom ministry. For the word does say, "the harvest is plenteous, but the laborers are few." And taking wrong assignments tend to simply exacerbate harvesting in ways that are not productive for the church.

As we delve further into the thinking of the "Chief" regarding the role of women in the Kingdom, let us take a peek at his book titled *Three Women, Sarah, Rebecca, Jezebel*. As opposed *to Apostolic Dilemma, Volume Two* that was penned in 1976, Three Women was done in 1993. Since Dr. Bonner is a progressive, futuristic thinker, that almost 20-year time span is worth examining. Maybe some new insight or revelation was made known to him.

The introduction to *Three Women* sets a very fascinating context. Mention is made of a past series taught on "Men In Mid-Life Crisis." then Pastor goes on to say that,

> (those) lessons dealt with the fact that many of our men are falling through the cracks because they are experiencing changes which affect their emotions and they don't understand how to deal with them. The consequence of their inability to deal with their emotions is broken homes. Many homes are destroyed by husbands walking out on their wives... This conduct is unacceptable and damaging to the wife.

At some later point, I hope to obtain a copy of that teaching series. But one important aspect of it is this. While some interpret Pastor's position on the women's role as "bashing women," it is important to know that he views with equal gravity and seriousness the role of the man in the Kingdom. This is especially true when he is reminding clergy about the awesome privilege and challenge to which we have been called. To know the man up close, one recognizes that the standards that he sets for himself are higher than anyone else with whom he associates or interacts. And he never accepts men who shirk their divinely appointed obligations.

It may well be true that some men in the ordained ministry are very intimidated by competent gifted and proficient women. And this insecurity may factor into their doctrinal positions about the woman's role. In my opinion though, one would be very hard pressed to prove such thinking in terms of Pastor Bonner's position.

Focusing again on the book, *Three Women*, notice what he states in the introduction as a basis for doing these lessons (the book <u>Three Women</u>).

> This... is an effort to bring to the surface the effect that women have on their families and the church. I selected... Sarah, Rebecca, and Jezebel, to demonstrate the attitudes and attributes of women who have had successful marriages and families.

Continuing in the introduction, additional comments are added:

> In order to save our families today... Look to the Word of God for guidance and to accept the manner of living set forth in Ephesians 5: 22-33.[18]

Considerable emphasis is placed on the responsibility of the husbands to love their wives. And this is not a lip

---

[18] William L. Bonner. Three Women: Sarah-Rebecca- Jezebel. New York: Greater Refuge Temple Publisher, 1993, p. 1.

service love. Neither is it a self-serving love. Rather, it is a love of respect and awe.

The Sarah Type

While describing Sarah, we are reminded that Abraham loved her greatly. And that love was expressed in such clear ways that Sarah knew without a doubt of her husband's love for her. When two people express agape love for each other in the intimate and holy setting of marriage, there is little they would not do for each other. Wasn't that surely the case with Sarah and Abraham?

> Sarah called Abraham 'lord' because she respected his rule. He had no need to beat her into submission.

> ... There was no requirement... That he be called lord, nor (did) his ego require such. But Sarah gave her husband this honor... In response to the love she received from Abraham.

This talk about Sarah's attitude was indeed unique. Apparently, this holy woman of God was very secure in who she was; so much so that she was willing to go to extraordinary efforts to please, satisfy, and fulfill Abraham. Note the rest of these comments:

She forfeited her rights of exclusivity as a wife and lowered her esteem as a woman. It was not at Abraham's demand nor was it due to his unfaithfulness that she permitted him to have her hand-maiden. Rather, she permitted it because she loved him and wanted him to be happy, complete and fulfilled.[19]

According to Pastor's opinion of Sarah, she had freely expressed a desire to please her husband. Additionally, these two precious individuals had some kind of romance going on.

We know that some of Sarah's decisions brought her discomfort and pain that pierced her heart deeply and profoundly, but part of that was due to their disobedience toward God. Once Sarah looked at her biological situation, she concluded that something had to be done for Abraham to have an heir. However, Sarah was wrong to offer Hagar to Abraham and he was wrong to accept her. As the "Chief" would say, a woman's efforts to please her husband must not go to the extent that she sins against God or damages her own life. And then he concludes by saying:

Abraham and Sarah (had) what I think to be an ideal type couple. They invested in each other, including the

---

[19] Ibid., p. 9.

important ingredients of love and romance. They had in place the glue that holds it together in abundance. [20]

The Rebecca Type

While Abraham fathered Ishmael with Sarah's maid, Hagar, he did later have a son with Sarah and that son, who became the heir, was Isaac. He was that child of promise, born when Abraham was 100 years old and Sarah was 90 years old. Thus, just as He said He would do, the Lord did it. It was not though, how or when the loving couple expected. It was simply in God's own time.

Some have speculated that next to the towering image of Abraham, Isaac seems to be lacking in some respects. Whether one agrees with that viewpoint or not, there is an area where Isaac did quite well. His choice of Rebekah as a wife has been lauded by some as one of his most pleasing accomplishments. That group includes the Bishop who was really impressed with the prayer life of Rebecca. It was in this area that he saw a difference between Sarah and Rebecca. Mother-in-law, Sarah made decisions and moved somewhat capriciously. Rebecca, though spent time with the Lord, seeking direction prior to making decisions. Rebecca had been like Sarah in that they both had experienced periods of barrenness. This had also been the case later with Rachel, the wife of Jacob, Samson's mother who was the wife of Manoah, Hannah, wife of Elkanah,

---

[20] Ibid., pp. 10-11.

mother of Samuel, and then Elizabeth, wife of Zacharias, and mother of John the Baptist. Each of these biblical women endured a time of being barren before the Lord blessed them and opened up their wombs to have children. This should remind us that one's current suffering is not always indicative of the end. Often it is the pathway that the Lord uses to lead us into future blessings.

In this case, one would think Rebecca felt her situation was going from one extreme to the other. After finally conceiving she realized that she was carrying twins and that a major disturbance was taking place inside her body. What she did next should trigger a key in all of God's people. Whenever there is a disturbance in the church body, one should seek the Lord before acting. Listen to the words in Genesis 25:21-24 (Modem Translation):

> Isaac pleaded with (God) to give Rebekah (Rebecca) a child, for even after many years of marriage she had no children. Then at last, she became pregnant. And it seemed as though children were fighting each other inside her:

> I can't endure this she exclaimed. So, she asked the Lord about it. And (He) told her, The sons in your womb shall become two rival nations. One will be stronger than the other; and the older shall be servant to the younger.

Her seeking the Lord is really what was so touching to Pastor. For he contends that sometimes the Lord will give the praying wife an insight, a revelation if you will, that the husband does not receive. The troubling nature of what was happening to Rebecca precipitated her seeking divine assistance. Giving us more enlightenment, the Bishop put it like this:

> Since this revelation was given to the wife… Rebecca was faced with a dilemma. She always sought to honor, obey, and please her husband, but now she was called upon to do what she knew he would not approve. There comes a time in life when a wife has to make a difficult decision. She should go to God for the answer to difficult decisions and be prepared to execute the solution given to her by God, whether the husband likes it or not. A wise husband will always give his wife the leeway that she needs to do things the way that God has revealed them to her.

For those who may think that this wise sage of a man expects women to <u>just</u> be servants to men, notice how he continues by saying:

> I find it so that when a husband is abusive and dictatorial to his wife, it is because he fails to understand that a wife too must do what God has given her to do. A <u>foolish</u> husband doesn't want

> his wife to do what God told her to do. He wants
> her to obey him... The husband is out of order
> and has superseded his authority. He has failed to
> understand that the Lord God speaks to both
> men and women, husbands and wives. [21]

This wise and godly woman received the necessities to implement the will of God without permanently offending Isaac. This serves as a glowing example that every wife (and every woman) needs to develop and nurture an intimate ongoing relationship with God. This can be so very helpful when the husband (or the man) becomes stubborn and wants to do what he thinks is right regardless.

So, what is it that stands out in the Rebecca type woman? First, she is a woman who has developed and continues to nurture a committed prayer life. This woman is mature emotionally and spiritually, in part because of the diverse circumstances and situations she has experienced. But she does not seek resolution separate from prayerful encounters with the Lord. The Rebecca type woman has long since understood that divine direction precedes human action.

Secondly, this type understands how to do the Lord's will while maintaining respect for her husband. When he does not pray consistently, he will often go off in the wrong direction. At those times though she knows what must be

---

[21] Ibid., p. 13.

done. Calling on her "divine connection" will enable her to get the necessary results.

The Jezebel Type

The last of these three women as created the major problem. The Jezebel type woman is far different from the other two. One probably would not find any of the traits and characteristics of Sarah and Rebecca in Jezebel, We are told that Sarah was considered by some to be the model wife and mother while Rebecca was viewed as prayerful and spiritual. But what about this woman Jezebel? Who was she, and what was she all about? In the words of Pastor, she was very domineering, and believed that she was on equal footing with the man. Not only could the man rule the woman, Jezebel felt that the woman could just as easily rule the man. If the man could be the head of woman, then it was also possible for the woman to be the head of man.

In the book *Three Women*, we are really given two perspectives on Jezebel. One was found in the Old Testament history of Israel; the other is from the book of Revelation as a so-called prophetess. The first is the wife of King Ahab recorded in I Kings; Chapters 18 and 19. This particular woman was the daughter of Ethbaal, King of Sidon (I Kings 16:29-33). The scriptures inform us that Ahab was bad enough, the worse king in Israel; and then he married Jezebel. As most know, her worship of idols was rapidly and freely accepted into the kingdom of Ahab.

So, we had the coming together of the worse king and his wicked bride; what a combination for Satan.

Once in a position of power and influence, Jezebel set out to weave her web of diabolical destruction. She tried to destroy all of the prophets of God, (I Kings 18:4) while promoting the prophets of Baal. She then "put out a twenty-four-hour contract," on the life of the holy man of God, Elijah, the prophet. Then when Ahab sought to obtain the vineyard of one named Naboth, the "sister" really went to work. Complicitous with the leaders of the city, she had Naboth killed by trumping up false charges against him (I Kings 21), and with the support of her "spineless" husband, wreaked hell and havoc on lives of the people in the Kingdom.

Apparently, the New Testament Jezebel was not much different. Her personality and priorities were right out of the playbook of her Old Testament namesake. That in itself is remarkable that the Lord would refer to her by the name Jezebel. That alone should have given cause to ponder how serious the Lord's message had to be. Notice what the Holy Word says to us in Revelation 2:19-23 (Modern Translation):

> I am aware of all your good deeds... also I know (of) your love, faith and patience... Yet I have this against you. You are permitting that woman Jezebel, who calls herself a prophetess to teach my servants that sex sin is not a serious matter; she urges them to practice

immorality... I gave her time to change her mind and attitude, but she refused. I will lay her on a bed of intense affliction... along with her followers... and unless they repent... I will strike them dead.

Two points are noteworthy to me here. First, Jezebel called herself a prophetess and did sinful teaching. But secondly, the pastor permitted her to do so. Those who are in leadership cannot just concede to anything in our local assemblies. There must be accountability to the Lord.

Let me close out this section by looking at the words of Pastor Bonner:

> These ministers created the same situation in the New Testament that the prophets created in the Old Testament... Do you know what God required for Ahab's children? He required that each of them be killed... When a thing is so evil that God requires its destruction by death in order to free a man or a people, it must be one of the most debasing things that a man can experience.[22]

As evil as the Jezebels were in scripture, that personality type has not left the church. There are Jezebels in charge of churches today. They have been placed in

---

[22] Ibid., p. 21.

positions as pastors, bishops, and apostles. This, however, is all man made, and contrary to the scripture." Statements like the preceding have been used by some to suggest that Pastor Bonner may not be objective when it comes to recognizing the contributions of women in the church. That viewpoint implies that anyone who disagrees with women serving in the ordained clergy is not fair or objective in his opinion of the female gender. In the church though, Bishop has clearly articulated his position within the context of scripture, not society. Perhaps looking at the women who participate in the ministries that God has given Pastor will be insightful. As I said earlier my professional experiences with him have come primarily through the W. L. Bonner College. In this ministry, women have been involved in very significant and important ways. During the twelve-year history of the college, two women have served as chairs of the College Board. They are Mrs. Raichelle Glover, and Mrs. Bridget Dewees. Also, Dr. Celeste Ashe Johnson serves as chair of the Academic Committee on the Board. In the College administration, Ms. Elaine McQueen is Director of Student Affairs and Administration. Ms. Tarshar Cunningham is Chief Fiscal Officer, while Ms. Natasha Davis is Administrative Assistant to the Registrar.

    Keep in mind that titles do not always accurately reflect one's job description. In particular Ms. McQueen and Ms. Davis, consistently perform a wide array of duties

WLBC. Also, the attorney for the International Church is Mrs. Jackie Stover-Stith, Esquire.

Therefore, one should not labor under the false assumption regarding the ministries God has given him: that "Women are to be seen and not heard." This simply does not apply to him. It should also be added, that this is not the only Christian ministry or denomination that takes this position on the biblical role of women. Others also contend that the role of the woman in the church is obsequious to that of the man. Having said that though, to know Pastor Bonner is to know that others do not lead him as it pertains to the Word of God. His own study, prayer, and direction from the Holy Spirit, determine what his positions will be on biblical issues.

Chapter 5
What About Your Emotions?

The foundation for this chapter is taken from the book that Pastor Bonner wrote titled *The Uncontrolled Emotions of Saved Young People*; with a publication date of 1977. When the word emotion is mentioned, so many thoughts may flood into an individual's mind. There are thoughts about who you are. Other thinking could revolve around your relationships with different people. What emotions come into play relative to various personal relationships? And how do they differ from emotions that surface relative to your professional and even casual relationships? When you read the Bishop's book, you will discover such interesting positions.

When one looks at the word emotion, what is it really? Some say strong feelings, others say feelings of passion such as love, hate, fear, or anger. Other words like sorrow, despondency, joy, happiness, lust, desire, shame, tenderness, and satisfaction may also be considered as emotions.

In his book, Pastor referred to his desire to teach on the subject of emotions. That desire was due to the complexity of emotional situations in which church people find themselves. Part of the responsibility of the pastor is to minister to the total needs of the people; the whole person "body, mind, and soul." It then requires those in the clergy to seek the appropriate training to be sufficiently prepared to minister to parishioners holistically.

A reason it seems necessary to know about emotions deals with the inclusive way we are impacted by them. I say this because in the book Pastor stated that:

> ... Our emotions usually determine whether we are good or bad, whether we curse others or pray for them. Our emotions determine whether we humble or exalt ourselves, whether we succeed or fail.

Quite frankly, as Stephen A. Smith would say, many never stop to consider emotions as being so pervasive in our make-up. Many just go about the business of life without a lot of mental introspection. But from Dr. Bonner's viewpoint, emotions are both dominant and powerful, for he continues:

> Our emotions determine whether we are happy nor depressed, whether we think positively or negatively. Our emotions determine whether we ever attain our goals in the academic, social, political or spiritual aspects of life. Our emotions determine it all. We are not as aware of this fact as we should be. If we could understand our emotions and how to deal with them,

we would be the stronger and the better for this understanding.[23]

Wow!! That is certainly a mouthful. The thing that grips me again and again is the progressive (sometimes out of the box) thinking of Pastor Bonner. Considered by many to be very traditional and conservative in his doctrinal thinking and his teachings, this book, I think, is an excellent example of his nontraditional thinking. One must again go back to the prevailing concepts in the mid 1970s. Few (if any other) Apostolic Organization's Presiding Bishops were delving into the role of emotions as to their effect on saved young people. It seems to me though because of the very strict teaching and various lists of "dos'" and "don'ts," any bishop in an Apostolic Church is imminently qualified to seriously consider the subject of emotions. One reason for making that statement grew out of a personal experience with my late loving father.

As a fourteen-year-old, I wanted so very badly to play basketball at my high school in Martinsville. When fall practice started, with a couple of friends, we decided to try out for the Junior Varsity team. Being freshmen, we did not think that we had the experience for the varsity just yet. Within a very short time, my coach and later very close

---

[23] William L. Bonner, The Uncontrolled Emotions of Saved Young People. New York: Greater Refuge Temple Publisher, 1991, pp. 9-10.

friend, the late Walter Massie, informed me that I had made the team. Well, with all of the excitement and glee that a young fourteen-year-old could have, I went home with the news. As soon as I finished telling my parents and sisters, my father told me that I had to quit the team. Surely you can imagine the low to which I crashed after all of my joy.

It was at that point that I turned to my mother and begged her to be my "intercessor" in this issue with my father. You see, Dad said that evening basketball practice and weeknight games would conflict with my attending weekly Bible study and choir rehearsal; and any other services that might take place. But, as it turned out, Mother knew my father much, much better than I. Her response was, "When your daddy's mind is made up, you will not be able to change it." So how can I say this? My emotions were "raw." I was severely depressed and devastated, to say the least. For the longest time, my desire was to stay as far away from basketball as I possibly could. It was simply too emotionally painful to observe.

All too well, I recall some of the feelings that I had. There was anger at my father and anger at the Church that would not allow me to enjoy a normal exciting youthful activity. While the resentment was stirring within me, the love and respect for my father remained. Needless to say, that young James C. Richardson, Jr. was an emotional, conflicted mess. Guilt topped the levels of emotions that I was experiencing.

Guess what? You can never imagine how that episode played out for me. Sometime after my twenty-first birthday, my father told me that he needed to talk with me. In that conversation, Dad really blew me away. He apologized for not letting me play basketball when I was 14 years old. And his words are still very clear in my mind. He said, "Son, at that time I pastored the way my pastor taught me." (His pastor was the late Bishop Eli Neal of the Saint Peters Church of God Apostolic in Winston-Salem, NC.) My father then said that everything he was taught to be sinful, was not a sin. So, his intent was to be more prayerful in trying to interpret and understand how the Bible addressed different subjects, during his time.

You know what? For many people reading this, they may not grasp the importance of that experience. However, for those who grew up in traditional Black Apostolic Churches before 1975 fully get the picture, and surely know whereof I speak. This experience, like so many others, has touched on the emotions of us in countless diverse ways. And rather than saying to young people they must accept something because he (the Bishop) said it, Pastor Bonner chose to explore, and then share with us the importance of understanding one's emotions.

If we are going to talk about emotions, at some point, we need to say a word or two about the word love. Doesn't it really epitomize the essence of emotions on so many levels? Listen to what Pastor Bonner says about it:

> ... love causes so much conflict in man. Yet it is a beautiful feeling although difficult to understand. Love expresses many things. Love can plunge one into turmoil, despair, depression, bewilderment, or it can lead one to a utopia of happiness, sweetness, and joy. Some people even commit suicide because of unrequited love... They find various other ways of destroying themselves, all because of unrequited love.[24]

Unrequited love is love that is not reciprocated. It is love that you have for someone on a level that the person does not have or is not showing toward you. Unrequited love results in people doing, at times, some strange things. It produces such a deep and penetrating hurt. You did not really start out to fall in love with that specific individual. There had been no prior discussion or conferences about developing a relationship on that level; no talk of an exclusive, monogamous arrangement. Yet, you now realize that feelings for that person just keep growing and growing. At the same time, the person for whom you feel and are

---

[24] Ibid., p.1.

expressing that love is not returning it to you. What a situation in which you find yourself; this dilemma can sometime lead to frustration and mixed emotions for the individual. He states:

> What brings true frustrations and mixed emotions is when one individual skips over (emotional stages). Circumstances may have pulled them out of the development of life, or they may have chosen to drop out. Now at a late age, they are discovering that because they skipped this, that and the other, they are unable to do (things). So now, they have to improvise... They are without the tools to deal with the problems of life... This creates emotional mix-ups.[25]

Contemporary American society has brought a much higher awareness to this subject of mixed-up emotions. Certainly, a primary reason this happens in young people, according to Pastor Bonner, is the awakening of emotions out of sequence. He contends that the first sign of awakened emotions is the appetite. Should one develop some desires prior to the certain maturity levels, there will be a lot of confusion. Unfortunately, persons as young as ten or twelve are having emotions come alive when they have absolutely no idea how to handle them. In far too many cases, these youth have turned to drugs, alcohol, and

---

[25] Ibid., p. 5.

sex. These vices have simply destroyed thousands way too soon. Lives are in disarray.

An example of this was brought to my attention just recently. A young lady, age fourteen or fifteen, was having a problem; although she did not think so. Because of her physical maturity, her appearance was that of a woman in her early twenties. But this was the problem. As opposed to having parents who should have protected her, this child's parents actually encouraged her into promiscuity. Yes, this story has been repeated thousands of times in urban, suburban, and rural areas around this nation. That, not withstanding, I am still petrified that parents openly tell their children it is fine to engage in sex. The young lady got pregnant, and now on top of dealing with so many confusing and conflicting emotions in her own being, she also has a new child for which to be responsible. Too young to be legal, she is now the parent of a new infant. Sexual desire, in this case, may not have developed in the way it did had it not been for the asinine and downright ignorance on the part of these parents. How wretched and contemptible were these parental examples, and how unfortunate was this child to have them as her primary examples of parenting. Could we call this example a case of emotional confusion passing from generation to another? It seems we either have to accept that or conclude that these parents were simply diabolical and evil. Focusing on people with mixed emotions, note what Pastor Bonner has to say,

Many times, the person in a mixed emotional state makes a serious mistake because common sense is thrown out the window... Whenever this happens, the young person is usually disappointed because emotional satisfaction is not always happiness... Then the experience brings with it the breaking up of morals, principles and virtues of life. Once... (these) have been destroyed, the strength of an emotionally stable individual weakens... If he becomes unstable in his (her) emotions, then he is in for a frustrating period in life that can last as long as he lives.[26]

No one should expect to go through life without encountering emotional frustrations and obstacles. Then what are we to do? In directing us to the scriptural verse, Saint John 6:35, the Bishop reminds us on what to build our lives.

And Jesus said unto them, I am the bread of life: he that cometh to me shall never hunger; and he that believeth on me shall never thirst.

---

[26] Ibid., p. 3.

Pastor makes poignant statements that give clarity to his point. Bread in the natural sense contributes toward the life and growth of the individual. He is using bread in a symbolic and substantive way. We must eat to live. Well, you must partake of Jesus Christ, He must be in your life and your mind in order to grow and have emotional stability. If we want the Lord Jesus in us, the Word has to be internalized. Someone said if we were to spend fifteen minutes a day reading the Word of God, the Holy Bible, we could read it through within a year. If you want to have your "equilibrium," then you must love Jesus, and you must eat, or partake of His Word.

The book, *Uncontrolled Emotions,* gives us the difference between "mixed emotions" and "sleeping emotions." Just as there is physical growth with chronological development, there is also mental growth. Some emotions only need to be awakened at certain ages and hopefully certain levels of maturity. When some emotions come alive or awaken before time, it can be confusing. The example of the fifteen-year-old girl showed emotions being awakened before she was mature enough to deal with and handle them. She then went from sleeping emotions to awakened emotions, to mixed emotions, and finally confused emotions. No matter what words she may have heard from "Jody," she really had no firm idea as to what she was getting into. What the young lady may have thought was love, was probably more akin to lust.

Love, though, is a profoundly strong emotion. It is one that most desire to experience at the "right time" in life. As a saved person, or a child of God, that emotion has to be guarded when awakened. There also needs to be someone who is reciprocating that love in a manner that is appropriate for two saved, but as yet unmarried people. If that does not happen, and only one person is in love, one enters the state that Pastor refers to as being in "limbo." By that, he means one person with awakened emotions that are not returned by the other party.

> Your emotions of love are fully awakened... become active, moving around. You start perspiring... when you see the other person, you become nervous and unsettled. The joy (and) gladness of seeing the person excites you. This is being in love... awakening one's sleeping emotions.[27]

If that love is not returned after one has reached the "in love state," what can be done about these emotions? I mean who really wants to do anything about those feelings? One's preference is to keep on having that joy and excitement. But the lack of reciprocity may lead to anger or resentment. So, the Bishop says some things here. First,

---

[27] Ibid., p. 16.

try not to fall in love too soon. This love usually leads to confusion. Thus, try not to fall in love with someone who is unable or unwilling to return that love. Try not to fall in love and get married if you do not have skills to provide for a productive marital relationship. For as beautiful as love is, it will not pay any bills.

Knowing that Pastor Bonner had done this publication some thirty years ago, I felt almost guilty asking him to resurrect his thinking at that time. Upon expressing that to him, he dismissed it as no big deal, and willingly agreed to an interview. The purpose of which was to get a more thorough understanding as to why he wrote on the subject of emotions and saved people.

This was a telephone conference. And there were initial pleasantries and mutual greetings exchanged prior to actually beginning the interview. That is mentioned because for me, it is always a joy and privilege to converse with this wonderful and precious Servant of God. Pastor possesses such amazing and profound wisdom, and he is so knowledgeable in many different fields and vocations. Further, he seems to constantly evaluate himself to see how he is doing relative to the agenda that God has for him. That is so evident by just looking at him and listening to him. At an age when most have been retired for a decade or two, he is looking for new challenges and opportunities to confront. And, apparently this has been his "modus operandi" for as long as people can remember.

Let us then go to the interview.

J.C.R., Jr.: You mention that awakening emotions out of sequence can create serious problems. Would you talk about how the Church needs to be aware of and address that problem? In other words, if a young person age thirteen to fifteen begins a relationship with an older person, what may happen?

Pastor Bonner: It is difficult for those whose emotions don't wake up until late in life to have control. Emotions are very strong. Because of this, young people must be encouraged to stay away from those activities that will awaken the wrong emotions too soon. The way to keep emotions asleep is through the power of positive thinking.

(For those who may be interested, Pastor Bonner has developed a two-semester class titled The Theology of Positive Thinking. It is a very exciting and dynamic class that you should consider taking.)

J.C.R., Jr.: You also mentioned in the book that uncontrolled emotions cause breakdowns in an individual's life. Can you give an example of that?

Pastor Bonner: When our emotions are out of control, we do things that we would not ordinarily do. And those things are usually the wrong things. So, it is important to keep our emotions in control, whether they are sexual, mental, physical, or spiritual. Keeping them under control is important.

J.C.R., Jr.: You said something that puzzled me somewhat. Which was, Jesus had to master His emotions. In what way did He have to do that?

Pastor Bonner: Jesus' emotions went out of control when He said to the Father, "if it is possible, let this cup depart from me." Jesus knew this cup could not depart from Him. He knew He had to drink it. But His emotions dictated what He was saying in His prayer, and what He wanted the Father to do. Jesus wanted the Father to do the impossible. That is the danger of following one's emotions.

J.C.R., Jr.: You wrote that David's emotions caused him to have a severed, a broken relationship with the Lord. Would you say more about that?

Pastor Bonner: David's emotions, out of control, caused great damage because he committed sin and murder. And the fact that he committed murder and took another man's wife, that caused him to lose favor with God for the rest of his life. So, when we follow our emotions and do the things that are so <u>damaging</u> to us spiritually, that's when we realize (sometimes) too late that living by one's emotions is dangerous. If I were to live by my emotions, I would be married tomorrow, but it would not be the right thing to do.

Upon reading page 45 in the book, Pastor Bonner reminds us of the urgent need to be filled with and know the working of the Holy Spirit as opposed to what we should do ourselves. He said we think the Holy Spirit is supposed to do everything, but there is something that we have to do.

J.C.R., Jr.: In the book, you stated that The Apostolic Church needs to teach on the office and work of the Holy Spirit and the office and work of the individual. Would you explain that more?

Pastor Bonner: There is a spirit in man. The Holy Spirit aids a person in finding the perfect and divine will of God for life. The knowledge of man is natural, is carnal, it is not spiritual, The spirit that is in man is (initially) not spiritual. So, he needs the aid of the Holy Spirit to control his spirit so that all the decisions that he makes will be under the guidance and direction of the Holy Spirit. (When this happens consistently, then we are not letting our emotions rule our decision-making process.)

J.C.R., Jr.: This is a quote from your book on page 50. "Your old life is put to death through the blood of Jesus Christ. But your emotions that are a part of your old life are controlled by the application of your faith and obedience to the work of God." Please share more on this.

Pastor Bonner: The natural man receiveth not the things of the Spirit, they are foolishness unto him. So, the old man is dangerous. And as long as he is alive within us, most of our decisions will be the wrong decisions. And most of the things we do will be the wrong things. It is so important to give the Holy Spirit the preeminence to control us totally. For he that is in the flesh cannot please God.

When people allow their emotions to control them, it prevents people from discovering the hidden things of God that need to be discovered; that need to be revealed. You must remember that Jesus had emotions. And emotions troubled Him at times. That's why He had to pray all night sometime. He continued in prayer all night. Now what was He praying for? You see He had emotions just like I have. He wanted steak just like I want steak. He wanted a woman just like I want a woman, but He had to say no, no, no, just like I have to say no. That is the power of positive thinking. Through the Holy Spirit, you can say no to anything and successfully get away with it.

J.C.R., Jr.: Near the end of the book, you talk about the stress that is on the pastor and the pastor's wife. What are two or three ways to deal with the stress that's on the pastor and the pastor's wife?

Pastor Bonner: The stress that is on the pastor and his wife goes like this. A pastor wants to be successful. He desires to be successful. He has this passion for success. He wants to pastor one thousand people, five thousand people. I want to pastor five thousand people and have succeeded in pastoring that many and more. But the stress that has come into my life, came about before I reached a level of spiritual growth where I could handle this kind of success. Now I can handle being pastor of ten thousand people or more because of my spiritual growth. (Now) my emotions are in total control that I don't feel about myself more highly than I ought to, because of my success. That is because I have learned from years of struggle with life how to succeed. And then after succeeding, control my emotions that can cause me to fall like "Humpty Dumpty off the Wall."

J.C.R., Jr.: I know it has been awhile since you have written this, but is there a point that comes to your mind about this book that was not a part of my questions? Is there another aspect of the book that you would care to share?

Pastor Bonner: (In addition to the comments that are listed in his Introduction, there was also another reason for Pastor Bonner writing this book.) I wrote the book because being the head of an organization like Church Of Our Lord Jesus Christ, which is a very large organization, I needed to supply information to the masses of this institution. I saw what was happening. I saw what was happening in the preacher that his emotions were out of control. I saw what was happening in the preacher's wife, her emotions were out of control. And when I saw this, I said Lord please help me to find a solution to the problem that is facing all of us. That's how that thought was conceived, and the Lord gave me the message *Uncontrolled Emotions*.

(End of Interview)

You know, even as I write these words, it is still somewhat phenomenal to me. After more than thirty years, Pastor Bonner can respond about his very specific writings in such a lucid and transparent way. The clarity of his mind is nothing short of miraculous. There is indeed something that is truly uniquely blessed and special about him.

Another point that is emphasized in the book is this. People especially saved people, and in particular young people must recognize and come to grips with their emotions. Understand that all of us must learn to master us. When that happens, decisions will not be made for all the wrong reasons.

As a part of a Father's Day sermon that I preached once, some attention was focused on Adam in the book of Genesis. I mentioned three things that were of interest to me regarding the life of Adam. Those things were his brilliant intellect, the special relationship that he had with God, and the way his mate (spouse) was given to him.

First, let me talk some about the intellect of Adam. According to Genesis 2: 19-20.

> So, the Lord God formed from the soil every kind of animal and bird, and brought them to the man (Adam) to see what he would call them; and whatever he called them, that was their name...

To me, that is mind blowing. Every single animal that you know about and all of those that you do not know about were given their names by one person. No university, college or department, no committee or special commission, no ad-hoc group participated in this process.

God alone created the animals and brought them to Adam, and he alone named them. What a level of intelligence Adam had to have. Can you ever grasp his imagination or level of creativity? Many may gloss over these verses, but I find them to be utterly exciting. No matter what flies in the sky, Adam named it. If it walks or crawls on the land, Adam named it. Yes, the Lord gifted Adam with a brilliant mind, but there was some self-cultivation that Adam had to do. Somebody once said your mind is God's gift to you. But the extent to which you will develop it, it is your gift back to God.

Next was the very special and close relationship that Adam had with the Lord. None of the animals that he named was able to provide substantive companionship. So, for a good while, Adam's "side kick" was the Lord. We don't fully know how long he was with the Lord prior to the creation of Eve. But can't you just visualize how awesome it was to "hang out" with Almighty God? Can you picture the special situations that arose for Adam to converse with our Creator? This was a uniquely precious and intimate relationship.

And then, thirdly, when God recognized Adam desired interaction with another human being, He personally made and delivered to Adam his bride. How many of us give serious time to fasting and prayer asking the Lord to give us whom He has for us, rather than who we want for a spouse? With all of the faith that we claim to have in the Lord, how many truly trust Him to hand deliver our spouse? Many of us will talk a lot of "ying yang" and say that we want the Lord to show us our life partner, but in reality, too many choices are decided on our emotions. And like Pastor Bonner said, love is a powerful, sometimes overwhelming emotion, that really becomes dominant when it is time to choose a mate.

Look, Adam, in spite of his mental brilliance, in spite of his close and personal relationship with God, allowed his emotions to lead him away from God. Didn't Pastor say for a saved person to rely on emotions can be a dangerous thing? How many people do you know (maybe you are one of them) who have made decisions for love that carried those individuals directly outside of God's will? That is exactly what Adam did. His mind told him to be obedient to God and not disobey his commands. But his emotions told him to please his wife, Eve. After she had eaten of the tree of knowledge of good and evil, she convinced Adam to do the same thing. He was in love, how could he not? He had stopped yielding to the Spirit of God and totally capitulated to the whims and desires of his wife. Hey y'all, Adam was in love, and his emotions took over!

There are some pretty heavy lessons to glean from this scenario. The emotion of love is simply too powerful for any of us to move in that direction without the leading of the Holy Spirit. Then we must pray daily and fast consistently to have the insight and the obedience to follow the Lord rather than our Own emotions. As the Bishop would say, we must learn who we are, knowing our strengths and weaknesses. Each of us has to know what we can confront, and what we had better avoid. Dealing with emotions is not a time to go into a state of denial, or, a fantasy. Emotions are very real. And only the Holy Spirit can help us deal with them in a way that is pleasing to the Lord. Quoting from the words of that English genius, William Shakespeare, Pastor Bonner said this:

> Everybody is looking for love (but)' to thine own self be true, and it must follow as the night, the day thou canst not then be false to whom? To any man... He that is true to himself cannot be false to any man... If you're true to yourself... if you don't tell yourself tales, if you don't tell yourself fantasies, if you face up to life with yourself, if you develop yourself fully, thou cannot be false to any man.
>
> ... Life can be charming. Life can be exactly what you're looking for. But to thine own self be true.[28]

---

[28] Ibid., p. 20.

Chapter Six
The Holy Spirit: Another Comforter

When one thinks long term about Pastor Bonner, you really begin to recognize the importance of his walk with the Lord. Spirituality to him is critically important. While others might feign interest in a deep spiritual life, it is no joke with Pastor Bonner.

Not too long ago, there were some ministers teaching on television. And one of their primary points was that the Holy Ghost or the Holy Spirit is not needed today. That was just for the first century church. Since we are blessed to have the Lord's word to study, the Holy Spirit is no longer needed. I shall never forget one of the minister's response to a telephone call from a viewer. She asked that TV minister, "Are you saved?" He said, "Yes." She asked, "Are you filled with the Holy Spirit?" He said, "No, and I don't need the Holy Spirit." At that response, something just shook in my spirit. A person who says that he is a minister of the Lord Jesus Christ, then blatantly and angrily, states that he and nobody else need the Holy Spirit in the 21st Century; well something is truly wrong with that.

The Lord even gave the Holy Spirit to select individuals in the Old Testament. Some got it before and others after He had given Moses the Law, the word for them to live by. So, even though the Lord gave to His people, His word and His Spirit in the Old Testament, according to these ministers, such is not the case m the New Testament. How interesting!!!

In the teachings by Pastor Bonner, we shall get a conclusive look at what it means to be Spirit filled and Spirit led. Our focus is drawn from two books that he has written. They are titled *Another Comforter* and *Life in the Holy Spirit.* Allow me to direct your attention first to the book, *Another Comforter.*

The title of this book is derived from the biblical passage in the fourth Gospel. St. John 14:16, "And I will pray the Father, and he shall give you another comforter, that he may abide with you forever." The modem translation says, "Then I will ask the Father to send you the Holy Spirit who will help you and <u>always</u> be with you."

This book evolved from lectures that Pastor Bonner shared with his telecast audience in Detroit during the year 1978. Part of the reason for the lectures came about because some were preaching and teaching in the Detroit area that the Holy Spirit is not necessary for salvation. In his discourse though, the Bishop said he would have us to know these very important comments,

> This important revelation of God through the Spirit to man is missing and must be sought after without delay. For without the Holy Spirit, we are not saved, we cannot survive, we cannot make the Rapture.

Going a step further, Pastor Bonner continues by saying:

> Jesus is telling His disciples that even though He won't be with them in the flesh, He will be with them in the Spirit to teach them all things.
>
> The Holy Spirit as a teacher can only work when He is dwelling in the life of an individual.[29]

Note the earlier part of the footnote where it states that "without the Holy Spirit, we are not <u>saved.</u>" The word saved, I have discovered is used in different ways by different Christian groups. Many use being saved synonymously with repentance or conversion. Some also say one is "saved, sanctified, and then Holy Ghost filled with the evidence of speaking in tongues." However, for many Oneness Pentecostals (Apostolics), repentance is merely the first step in the Salvation process. But one is not saved until you are filled with the Holy Spirit. The point being, how can one experience Spiritual rebirth, apart from the Holy Spirit? That is, what causes one to be saved; and then live a life that is Christ centered and pleasing to the Lord.

---

[29] William L. Bonner, Another Comforter, Detroit, MI: 1978, p. 3.

Most of us are aware that many in the Christian Church in America use the scriptural verse, Romans 10:9 as, what some call, a foundational verse for salvation. Well, there are at least two problems with doing that. First, the writer of Romans believed by many to be the Apostle Paul, had not even gotten saved when several thousand in Jerusalem experienced that wonderful new birth. So, they could not be told, "That if thou shalt confess with thy mouth the Lord Jesus, and shalt believe in thine heart that God hath raised him from the dead, thou shalt be saved." Many in Jerusalem had experienced salvation before the writer of Romans was saved and then later penned this epistle. Naturally the question begs, how did the Jerusalem crowd of well over five thousand know that they were saved? They certainly did not use Romans 10:9 as their reference.

Then secondly, the word confess in scripture has more than one meaning. In that regard, it is like the word love. Confess means to repent, but it also means to proclaim. For example, a couple has decided to enter into an exclusive courting relationship, but no public announcement of that has been made. However, every time you see them around each other there is glow, there is unbridled happiness. Finally, someone says to one of them, "You are in love. Every time that other person is in your presence, you light up like a Christmas tree." With a burst of enthusiasm, and jubilant release, the persons joyously proclaim, "You are right. I must confess that I am in love."

This person is not repenting, this person IS proclaiming, because there is no sin here.

What then was the situation regarding Romans 10:9? Was Paul telling sinners what they needed to do to be saved? The writer of Romans was saying to Jews who had turned from the Law and accepted Jesus as Lord, that now was the time to speak up and proclaim it so that other Jews will know that they too needed the Lord Jesus Christ. The Roman writer wanted the Jewish converts to know that now was not a time to be shy, timid and bashful. Rather it was time to proclaim what the Lord had done in them, and for them. It occurs to me that some today need to express themselves with Holy boldness and say, "I am saved because the Lord has filled me with His precious Holy Ghost.

According to Pastor Bonner, those who reject the Holy Spirit in actuality are really rejecting Christ;

> There are many clergymen who do not teach the reception of the Holy Spirit by all believers. As a result of the absence of the Holy Spirit, our churches are overrunning with sinners... The pulpit(s) and the pews.

Continuing, Pastor Bonner gets to what he really sees as the crux of the matter.

> On that day (Pentecost) they were all filled with the Holy Ghost and began to speak with other tongues as the Spirit of God gave them the utterance. Of course, this is the controversial aspect of the Holy Spirit or Comforter, speaking in other tongues.[30]

It has been rightly stated that confusion exists regarding the whole issue of tongues. Those who teach against it, labor under some confusion as well as those who say that they believe in it. But listen as he gives divinely inspired insights on this very important issue.

> The fulfillment of prophecy relating to tongues had come (on the Day of Pentecost. Joel 2:28, Isaiah 28: 11, Mark 16:17)[31]

He further contends that you cannot separate the Holy Ghost from tongues, because the tongues are evidence that the Holy Ghost has come into the life of the believer. We are then cautioned about speaking against the Holy Spirit because there may be something that is <u>unclear</u> to a particular individual. At those times, people should diligently seek the Lord in prayer to see if the Spirit has more information to give us. All too often, folk will allow tradition to dictate what we have always believed is what

---

[30] Ibid., p. 4.
[31] Ibid., p. 4.

we must believe now. One of Pastor Bonner's concerns is that people will not be guilty of blaspheming against the Holy Spirit in their ignorance or close mindedness.

Why is so much importance attached to speaking in tongues when one receives the Holy Spirit in what we call "living under Grace?" According to the Bishop, "God uses signs to distinguish His people. Under the Law, it was circumcision. Under Grace, it is speaking in tongues." In each instance, the Lord, and not man, determined what the sign would be. Old Testament Israel did not just do circumcision for those who were a part of the initial group and stop. The act of circumcision was still in existence when Jesus was born. You do recall Mary and Joseph carrying Him to the temple for the ritual. So, if the Lord initiates or decrees something, only He can determine who says when it is no longer proper and appropriate. It seems that the New Testament Church acknowledged and believed that speaking in tongues was appropriate at one time, but not today.

Let us go further into this discussion because our Bishop has much more to share. Speaking parabolically, he compares the Bible to the United States Constitution. No department of the government, or any single state, has the authority to change or modify the Constitution. The U.S. Congress (Senate and House) may initiate legislation related to amending the Constitution, but then it must be ratified by a majority of the 50 states, to become official. Short of that, it simply will not happen.

When it comes to the Bible that principle also applies.

> ... It is important... to understand that you cannot change God's Word whenever you see fit... Be it (the) bishop or pope. Who can change that? No one except those whom authority is given to make changes. Article One in the Bible states 'Go ye therefore, and teach all nations, baptizing them in the name of the Father, and of the Son, and of the Holy Ghost' (Matthew 28: 19). This is Article One in the Constitution of the Christian Family.

Look, though at how the he expands on those words, by giving us more knowledge, and a better understanding.

> Now what is the name of the Father, the Son, and the Holy Ghost? The name of the Father is Lord (Isaiah 42:8). The name of the Son is Jesus (Luke 1 :31). The name of the Holy Ghost is Christ (I Corinthians 10:4).

> His full name is Lord Jesus Christ and it is in this name that one must be baptized. No one has the authority to change this article, no preacher, no bishop, no one.

Even as we focus on baptism in the Spirit, this scripture has been a source of contention between

Trinitarians and Oneness (Apostolics) believers in the church for many, many years. In the understanding of the Oneness believers, this scripture was never meant to be a formula for water baptism. Instead, it is a part of what a goodly number has come to refer to as the <u>Great Commission.</u> Our Lord Jesus Christ had authorized His followers to prepare to evangelize the world. This scripture is also recorded in the book of Saint Mark with slightly different wording.

> And he said unto them, Go ye into all the world, and preach the gospel to every creature. He that believeth and is baptized shall be saved; but he that believeth not shall be damned. (Mark 16: 15-16)

Oneness followers do not believe anyone has been baptized (in water) in the name of the Father, Son, and Holy Ghost, unless the name is used. That is why when baptism takes place, it should be in the name of the Lord Jesus Christ. This point is substantiated by the fact that biblical baptism always occurred using the name. (Please read the book of Acts.)

Next, we are given the second important mandate that the church needs to follow:

> Article Two is in St. Mark 16:17, 'And these signs shall follow them that believe; In my name shall they cast

out devils; they shall speak with new tongues.' Just as you cannot change the (U.S.) Constitution (arbitrarily) you cannot change the Articles of the Bible... Now those... who say that the tongues didn't go beyond the Day of Pentecost are wrong.

... After that the Holy Ghost fell... around Jerusalem, Palestine, Asia, Europe, Egypt, and Ethiopia.[32]

In addition to the Holy Spirit falling in Jerusalem on the Day of Pentecost for the Jews, the Bible gives other examples of this blessed experience. These accounts in the book of Acts are so very important because this is our primary New Testament Book of History. Once events are put into the historical archives, we can speculate, opinionate, agree or disagree, but we cannot change them. More than a few have tried to alter history by embellishing points to suit their fancy, but history is just what it is.

On the day of Pentecost after the first one hundred twenty had this life changing experience, they were shortly joined by three thousand more converts. That number in turn rose to over five thousand by chapter four of Acts. When we get to chapter eight, we see Philip ministering in Samaria. The exodus from Jerusalem had been motivated in part by the senseless and shameless murder of a holy man named Stephen. Upon arriving in Samaria, Philip was

---

[32] Ibid., p. 20.

greeted by a very receptive group, who got baptized in water in the name of the Lord Jesus. And, subsequent to the debarkation of the Apostles, this ready group of members was filled with the Holy Spirit. (Acts, Chapter 8)

Now the reason we conclude that speaking in tongues accompanied their receiving the Holy Ghost is something radically different happened. Earlier in the chapter, the Lord had used Philip's ministry to heal the sick and cast out demons (unclean and evil spirits). They had also seen Simon use sorcery or witchcraft to do unusual things. Because of the extraordinary things he did, the people assumed (though wrongly) that Simon was a man of God. This episode emphatically points to the dire importance for one to be filled with the spirit and then maintain a consistent relationship with our Lord. Without Him (the Spirit) people can do things that "appear" or "seem" like they are doing God's work. When the people received the Holy Spirit, even Simon observed something that was different from Philip's ministry and very different from his own distorted works. We believe what Simon observed was the people in Samaria speaking in tongues as they were filled with the Holy Spirit. This happened while Peter and John were ministering to them.

At least two other instances in the Acts of the Apostles deserve some attention. The first is in the tenth chapter. One named Cornelius, a Gentile, desired a closer relationship with the Lord. The Holy Word indicates that he was a devout and sincere man who had great reverence for God. Note, while the Spirit prepared Cornelius to receive Peter, the Spirit also prepared Peter to preach to Cornelius and his household. During that sermon, the Holy Spirit filled them as they spoke in tongues. The second instance is recorded in the 19th chapter of Acts. Paul encountered some disciples of John the Baptist, who, like Cornelius, wanted to know more about the Lord. Also like the Cornelius Family, not only did they get baptized in water in the name of the Lord Jesus, they also received the Holy Spirit while speaking in tongues.

Perhaps though, it is not in the book of Acts that so many conflicting views emerge regarding the issue of speaking in tongues. Instead one would suspect that it is in I Corinthians that one finds information which has led to the growth of such divergent opinions on this unsettling subject to many. In this book, the Apostle Paul never once condemned speaking in tongues. The point that he wanted to convey to the Church at Corinth, was for them to learn and understand the proper use of tongues. In the 14th chapter of I Corinthians, verse 2, it states, "For he that speaketh in an unknown tongue speaketh not unto men, but unto God: for no man understandeth him; howbeit in the Spirit he speaketh mysteries."

Knowing that sometimes the King James Version is just a little difficult to understand, let's read that verse again in a modem translation. "If your gift is that of being able to speak in tongues, you will be talking to God but not to others, since they won't be able to understand you. You will be speaking by the power of the Holy Spirit, but it will all be a secret." If what is being said is a secret or a mystery, then what is the purpose?

Nobody will understand. Listen to Pastor Bonner elaborate with clarity.

> I Corinthians 14:4 says 'He that speaketh in an unknown tongue edifieth himself, but he that prophesieth edifieth the church.'
>
> You see, speaking in an unknown tongue is for individual edification. It is something between God and man. It is not for man to express to others for some spiritual benefit or spiritual edification. It is a language used by God, given to the individual to communicate with God in a personal way... But he that prophesies, edifies the church, strengthens the church... Paul isn't condemning those that speak in unknown tongues, but he is merely saying which has the most profit to the church.[33]

I Corinthians, Chapter 3, talks about the importance of Christians growing to a state of spiritual maturity; going from the "milk" to the "meat." Well, when it comes to speaking in tongues, he reminds us that there needs to be

---

[33] Ibid., pp. 23-24

maturity demonstrated in the church. He states that there were some problems in the Corinthian group. However, the presence of problems did not then and do not now negate the importance of speaking in tongues as the sign of Holy Spirit baptism. We learn from the Word that people can be zealous for certain spiritual gifts because of what it may do for them. Some people actually try to present themselves in a posture that suggests that they are very deep and holy spiritually. But there are further instructions.

> Paul regulates the tongues in the 10th and 11th verses of I Corinthians, 14th chapter... People speaking in tongues and nobody understands what they are saying is a confusing situation. There should be order to tongues in the church... 'Even so ye, forasmuch as ye are zealous of spiritual gifts, seek that ye may excel to the edifying of the church' (verse 12).[34]

My understanding of these comments is that every child of God should seek spiritual gifts that benefit the whole congregation, not to engage in emotional activities trying to impress those in the local assembly. So as much as one may enjoy speaking in tongues, it needs to be kept in perspective; be mindful of what the priorities are in Chapter 14. The primary gift is prophesying. Just like

---

[34] Ibid., p. 25.

preaching the Gospel is more important than singing in the worship, that also is the case with speaking in tongues and prophesying.

Let us just look at that word just for a moment. Prophesy. What does it mean? In the Old Testament, the prophet was one who received and declared a word from the Lord, and it was done by the leading and direction of the Holy Spirit. The prophet of God was an anointed and consecrated Servant, whose message was never his own, it was always the Lord's doing. One of the things that he learned was his speaking was not always popular or well received. An example comes to mind of Prophet Micaiah, whose story is recorded in II Kings, chapter 22. Just a bit of a summary: King Jehoshaphat of Judah and King Ahab of Israel were forming an alliance to stand against Syria and its king. Prior to moving forward, Jehoshaphat wanted to hear a word from the Lord. After hearing from Ahab' s fur hundred heathen prophets, the King of Judah specifically requested to hear from "a prophet of the Lord." Ahab mentioned Micaiah, but prefaced his comments by saying that prophets' declarations were always gloomy. But the fact of the matter was, Micaiah did not say what Ahab wanted to hear, because he said what God mandated. And, since the King of Israel was living outside of the will of God, the message was not pleasing to him. While the prophet may speak with concern and compassion, he must speak what the Lord has given him to say. And it may not always be pleasing to the hearer. But if the hearer obeyed what was said, he would always be blessed and not cursed. Thus, the Old Testament prophet really had as a major focus foretelling what was to be.

In the New Testament, there is another way of looking at the word prophesy. In addition to foretelling future events, the word is also defined as to proclaim. That definition is very close to the meaning of the word preach. Some have postulated on this because the New Testament Church in the first century did not have a written word, other than the Old Testament. Consequently, the belief was that the Holy Spirit would frequently give new revelations to the infant church. When that occurred, it was considered prophesying. Indeed, that blessed the entire congregation or local assembly.

Toward that end, Paul wanted the Corinthians to recognize that while speaking in tongues may edify the individual, prophesying blessed the whole congregation. When it happened, unless the Lord already had an interpreter in the group, the prophecy was in the language or dialect of the people.

With Pastor Bonner, one of the blessings of his teachings is the concise understanding that he conveys to the student or listener.

> "Note the 23rd and 24th verses, 'If therefore the whole church... came together into one place, and all speak with tongues... This is confusion.

> ... but if all prophesy and there came in one that believeth not, or one unlearned, he is convinced of all, he is judged of all. Prophesying in tongues is important if there is an interpreter. If there is no interpreter, then there should be no prophesying.
>
> ... The Corinthian Church was confused, mixed up because everybody was doing his own thing. Everyone was in the tongue syndrome... This was chaos in the congregation.[35]

Rather, than taking the time to seek an understanding to share with the people, other ministers have just taken the position that speaking in tongues is not supposed to be for today. But our Chief Apostle gives us knowledge and wisdom that was poured into his mind by the Holy Spirit, and helps us to better comprehend and grasp the whole doctrine on speaking in tongues. On page 26 in the book of *Another Comforter*, Pastor warns against the misuse of the tongues in worship.

> Just because you have the tongues in your life, you shouldn't seek spiritual ecstasy *in expressing these humanly* (my emphasis). They should always be <u>*expressed divinely*</u> (my emphasis) ... always giving

---

[35] Ibid., p. 27

yourself to the leading of the... Spirit of God. If this is done, the Church will not be confused about tongues.

During a conference that I attended in the past, an interesting occurrence happened in one of the worship experiences prior to the choir starting to sing. All of a sudden, we heard this talking as if someone were prophesying. Several pastors in the pulpit motioned for the choir director to just ignore the person and move ahead with the song. I could see that the director was puzzled and confused. I could also see that while we as clergy were making comments from our pulpit seats, for the most part, we did not know what needed to be done. It was at that time that I went to the podium, told the brother he was out of order and called for the song.

Now, in no way, did I want to disrespect or embarrass the brother who was speaking. But if he could just stand up at any point in the worship and start talking, what was to keep others from following him and doing the same thing? If there is to be order, then such a person should speak to the pastor or the bishop and share what the Lord has told him. Then a decision can be made about how it should be handled

In a preceding footnote, Pastor Bonner used the term spiritual ecstasy. What does that word mean? It is a state or feeling of overpowering joy, rapture, a state of being beyond reason and self-control. When it comes to speaking in tongues, I believe Pastor Bonner is saying we are not out of control if the Spirit is doing it. Added to this, we are given more instructions by the Bishop.

> It doesn't speak well for the Apostolic Church to have such disorder. Tongues bring you into the Church so that we know we are in the Body of Christ. After we come into the Church, tongues should be regulated according to the Word of God. Tongues were never used by the early Apostolic Church as they are being used today. There is nowhere in the history of (the) Apostolic Church that after you receive the Holy Ghost and spoke in tongues that tongues became a way of life in the congregation.

Continuing with some more instructions we are told that:

> Tongues bring you into the church and afterwards, tongues come as a refreshing from God. God pours out His Spirit upon the congregation. They receive a refreshing and sometimes they speak in tongues. But that is not a long duration. It is just for the reviving and refreshing of the congregation. The point of confusion is the way tongues are being utilized in the church today that causes unbelievers to say that you are mad. You don't know what you are doing! The unbeliever wants to hear the Gospel! He wants you to tell him your story in a language that he can

understand. That is exactly what Jesus Christ wants of us. Every Child of God should present God in the most intelligent way possible.[36]

Interview with Pastor Bonner

J.C.R., Jr.: I like to turn now to your book, *Life In the Holy Spirit*. Reading your books, has been absolutely inspiring. I have really enjoyed them.

When you talk about life in the Holy Spirit, there were three words that you used to describe the Spirit's relationship with a person in the Old Testament. My question is, other than speaking in tongues, and the Spirit being given to select individuals, as opposed to who so ever will, in the church age, what is different about the Holy Spirit in the Old Testament and in the New Testament?

Pastor Bonner! There isn't any (major) difference. The difference is how He worked in the Old Testament and how He works in the New Testament. It was the Holy Spirit (back then) but he just worked in a different way. For instance, in the New Testament, the Holy Spirit causes the believer to speak a foreign language. In the Old Testament, that was not given to man through the Holy Spirit. The Bible says the righteous men spoke as they were moved by

---

[36] Ibid., p. 29.

the Holy Spirit, the preachers, the prophets. Alright, now in the New Testament, we possess it. Everybody possesses the Holy Spirit, not just the prophet, preacher, but everybody in the congregation, which means the Holy Spirit brings everybody up on the same level.

You have members in the congregation who can see further than the preacher in the pulpit; which means that person in the congregation has permitted the Holy Spirit to function to operate in her life or in his life, that they have risen to a level where they know more than the pastor knows. And the pastor, instead of rising to the level that he can become the tiffany of the leadership of his congregation, has become more carnal than spiritual. Then he sees God working more through his members that God is doing through him. And that is a dilemma. For the Bible says how can they hear without a preacher, how can he preach except he be sent?

J.C.R., Jr.: Alright. This next question focuses on prophesying and how should that be understood relative to the gift of interpretation?

Pastor Bonner: An interpreter is one who has an understanding of what is needed to be said. So, what is said is done so because of what is needed at that (particular) time. And the individual, through the Holy Spirit understands that. So what God does through the tongues expression is take over the person, and the person will prophesy or say things when he is not on that level (normally), the Spirit is using that person. But as soon as the Spirit finishes using that person in that form, the Spirit leaves him (like that) and the person comes down to a lower level. But when the person is prophesying, he is on a level that he does not live on every day.

J.C.R., Jr.: On page (7) in your book, you made a statement that we should want the Holy Spirit to have total control of our lives so that we might receive the *ultimate blessings*. When you say or use that phrase, *"ultimate blessings,"* what do you mean other than eternal life?

Pastor Bonner: Alright. Eternal life is a gift—the gift of eternal life. Everybody that is saved is going to have that, which some day we are going to live forever. But that part has nothing to do with what the Holy Spirit is all about (in another aspect). That life (eternal) is a gift from God. You don't have to be on the third level to have eternal life. You don't have to be on the tenth level; you can be in the basement and have eternal life. Alright—but the Holy Spirit takes us to different levels, you see. Like John (said) I was in the Spirit on the Lord's day. Now, what John saw in the Spirit in the book of Revelation, was different from what Peter saw. Peter had the Holy Ghost speaking in tongue just like John had. But Peter couldn't see what John saw. John could see the end of time, he could see the Great Tribulation, the Battle of Armageddon, the things that are going to happen; he could see all those things. Through what? The eyes of the Holy Spirit. Now the Holy Spirit in the life of a preacher makes it possible for that preacher to reach levels that he never thought it was possible to reach.

Take, for instance, I am a successful preacher. I pastored as many as fifteen churches at one time. And my churches are not empty; they are full of people. Why it is because of the level that I live on through the power of the Holy Spirit. Any preacher can have the same success that I have had, but they will have to allow the Holy Spirit to take them to the "third heaven" or the "second heaven," or the "first heaven," so that they feel things and see things that they never saw before; and then apply those things. I have applied in my life those things that the Holy Spirit has enabled me to understand, so that the end result is my churches are full of people and other pastors have churches that are half empty or one third full.

It is important, as many as are led by the Spirit of God, they are the Sons of God. I can't emphasize that enough. Every preacher can be a Bonner and have the William Lee Bonner success, and even more. I am 85 years old, and I am still looking for success. I don't have the real success that I want yet. I want more, I want more, and I am going to have it; I'm going to achieve it.

J.C.R., Jr.: Pastor Bonner, just listening to you—your life is such an inspiration, and what a noble example for others of us in the ministry to follow. Let me now shift for a moment and look at another exciting aspect of your life. In terms of special gifts, when did you become aware that you had the gift of construction, being able to build with such artistry, because you say that you never went to school (to learn how to develop these building skills)?

Pastor Bonner: When I left the farm, I told my daddy to take his plough and his mule. Then I went to the House of the Lord and turned my life over to the Holy Spirit. And when the Holy Spirit came into my life, I discovered at that point in time that I could be a successful man, and I became a success as a young man. I wasn't old then, I was young; but I knew that God had something better for me; and all I needed to do was to allow the Holy Spirit to work through me and to bless me.

Bishop Lawson discovered that God had given me something that He didn't give young people ordinarily. This gift that I had was not in a lot of young people, but God gave it to me. And as a result, I have become the Chief Apostle Of the Church Of Our Lord Jesus Christ. Praise the Lord now, I am looking for something else to be.

J.C.R., Jr.: Now you mentioned that even though many will seek with sincerity and commitment to know the deep things of God, that everybody will not know the deep things of God. For example, you talked about the fact that even though Daniel and the three Hebrew Boys prayed, only Daniel got the understanding about the dream of Nebuchadnezzar (the book of Daniel, Chapter 2). If the three Hebrews were as committed and as sincere as Daniel, what determined, or why is it that they could not, or did not get the same kind of understanding as Daniel got? And why does that happen today if several individuals are all as committed in their walk with the Lord, but some will get an understanding of the deep things of God and some will not?

Pastor Bonner: God has given millions of men the Holy Spirit. Some of these men have a deeper understanding. All of these men are not on the same level. I am looking at the twelve Apostles in the Church Of Our Lord Jesus Christ, and they are good men. But I want them to come up to higher levels in preaching, thinking, living— higher levels. I am looking at them, and I believe if they would spend more time with me in a classroom, like the W.L. Bonner College *(laughter by Bishop Bonner)*, they would also rise to other levels.

You would be surprised how far you can go in God when you put together a combination of positive thinking, and a prayer life, a life of fasting, a life of meditation, a life of dedication. Put a combination of these things together, you are bound to go to the top.

J.C.R., Jr.: Well, is it your understanding that this is what Saint Paul did, as opposed to Saints Peter, James, and John?

Pastor Bonner: Absolutely, absolutely. Paul is a "Johnny come late." He wasn't among the Apostles when Jesus was here (on earth as a man). He never heard Jesus teach anything. The Apostles heard Jesus teach <u>day and night</u> but look what happened to Paul. He came out of the woods (desert), you know, and went to the top; became the Chief Apostle. Even the (other) Apostles admitted that Paul had written things that were hard to be understood.

J.C.R., Jr.: When you talk about the steps that one must take for the Holy Spirit to open up your mind and make you skilled at collecting knowledge, what is it that we need to do?

Pastor Bonner: Fast and pray.

J.C.R., Jr.: Shifting just a little bit, on page 31, you make a point that Blacks are tolerated by Whites, but not accepted by Whites. Yet, Blacks want to, as a way of showing our success, when we are doing better economically, some Blacks try to get a house in their neighborhood; and as a part of that you said that even after Whites have received the Holy Spirit, many of them still have to wrestle with their racism. What is your position about this now?

Pastor Bonner: The same, the same. That racist demon is; it is not just a theological belief related to their interpretation of the Bible. They were told a lie about Black people; that Black people are inferior. That's a lie. Alright. You know what the Bible says about believing a lie and being damned? That's the White Man. He has believed a lie and is damned for it. He is so damned for the lie that he has believed that he cannot accept Black people on the same level with White people; in this hour in time, he still can't accept it.

I preached for White pastors and I see them struggling with trying to accept me. I see this. I used to preach for a well-known White pastor in Tennessee. And he used to preach for me. When I went down to Tennessee, that pastor would say, we don't believe quite like you do. He said when you pray for the White women (in the congregation), don't put your hands on them. I asked him, why? The Bible says they shall lay hands on the sick, and the sick shall recover. If your people are sick, the Lord can heal them through me. He said this is the south, this is the south. Now here is a noted evangelist, who has not risen above racism. Racism is a demon, and it is a demon that most White folk have not cast out yet.

J.C.R., Jr.: While we are talking about demons—I had this later, but let me go ahead and ask it now. Could you talk more about the difference between flesh demons and satanic demons?

Pastor Bonner: Sure. I have flesh demons (but) I don't have satanic demons. I have flesh demons in me. Alright, if we live after the flesh, the Bible says, you shall die. But if you, through the Spirit, do mortify the deeds of the body, you shall live. Flesh is a demon. He is not satanic, he is flesh, flesh. And we accede to the fact that this flesh demon is in control of so many things. That's why saints can commit adultery, saints can commit fornication, that's why saints become lesbians, that's why saints become homosexuals, because they are in the flesh, they are not in the Spirit. That's why (some) pastors can't rise to a level of success that they want in their lives because they have a flesh demon. He won't let them pray. He won't let them fast. He won't let them study the Word of God. So, the flesh demons are in control in the church in so many areas that it is pathetic; because people don't know that they have a demon called flesh. That's why some sisters can slap the face of other sisters and brothers can curse out other brothers because they have a demon of the flesh that is not under control.

J.C.R., Jr.: How does one in terms of the manifestation of it then—or is it possible for a flesh demon to open the door to the heart of an individual for a satanic demon to come in?

Pastor Bonner: Oh yes, absolutely.

J.C.R., Jr.: This is a quote from page 39. "What you feel makes you happy only to a certain point, but what you know makes you happier. You have the Holy Ghost which makes you happy, but knowledge makes you happier. Knowledge IS something that broadens (the person).

My question is, how does knowledge give you more happiness than the Holy Ghost?

Pastor Bonner: Knowledge is something that you have acquired. You have the Holy Spirit, but you will not allow it to function in your life the way it would like to function. But knowledge, for most people, is one of their greatest assets. When you have knowledge, you have acquired something that makes you proud of who you are, and makes you proud of life. It has that positive effect on the individual. My knowledge makes me feel extremely good. The Holy Ghost makes me feel good when the Holy Ghost is working in me. But it isn't every day that the Holy Spirit is working like that. But every day, I can use knowledge because I have it. And I use knowledge more than I use the Holy Spirit. And, I think God approves of that. I believe He approves of that because I am who I am because I have knowledge, as well as the Holy Spirit. But the knowledge that I have of people, of different philosophies, it's absolutely fantastic, you know.

J.C.R., Jr.: Sometimes I feel like I am being unfair to you. Because of my recent reading of this material (your books), it is fresh in my mind. In your case, though, it has been a good while since you wrote this.

Pastor Bonner: A long time ago *(with laughter)* I need to write another book.

J.C.R., Jr.: That would be wonderful. There was another page when you talked about the need for us to spend time in prayer and meditation. What is your method that has gotten you on the (spiritual) level that you are? Obviously, it is higher than most ministers, well it is higher than any minister that I know.

Pastor Bonner: Prayer, fasting, meditation. I spend at least three to four hours at different times during the day in prayer. Since noon today, I spent about one and a half hours in prayer. At three different intervals—some of my prayer periods are one hour—some are half hour. But I never pray less than thirty minutes. I never pray, say five minutes and I'm gone. It takes time to get into the

Spirit of travail that brings forth the impossible, that reveals the impossible. I enjoy it.

I actually enjoy my prayer time. It is absolutely enlightening, delightful, and dynamic.

J.C.R., Jr.: How long have you had that kind of enjoyment with your prayer life in the Spirit?

Pastor Bonner: Years. It has been years. I've been this way for years. I could not have had the success that I have had without a prayer life; it is impossible. I could have done this in the flesh. I would be like many (other) ministers and still just have fifty members.

J.C.R., Jr.: In preparing your teaching, preaching, counseling, preparing for building, it is obvious that you spend a great amount of time with the Spirit. In terms of your preaching and teaching, what place do commentaries, Bible dictionaries, and other resources have in your preparation process as opposed to your prayer life? I know when I am teaching a class in preaching, I tell my students if you look in the commentary, it will give, in most instances, what is considered the standard interpretation of the scripture. But you still have to go to God in prayer to see what the Spirit says about that. How much time do you spend reading as opposed to praying in preparation for preaching and teaching?

Pastor Bonner: I don't spend as much time reading as I do praying. I spend more time praying than I do reading. Alright. I have done a lot of reading. Don't misunderstand me, but what the Holy Spirit has taught me has taken me into deeper things of life; the deeper things of life that dictionaries and commentaries won't give me. And I think: when ministers take commentaries and use them in the place of prayer—then they say I've got an understanding because (this or that) commentary says so. I go beyond the commentary. I see what they have to say, but go beyond that, and ask the Lord, what is it that you want me to understand? What is it? Take me into the mysteries of your will and your purpose. Show me, show me Lord. When I am praying all these prayers, I am asking for knowledge. All the knowledge that I have—it seems that a man who has acquired all the knowledge that I have should be satisfied, but I am not. I want more, I want more knowledge. I want to be head and shoulder above every preacher. *(laughter)* That's what I want. Am I wrong? I don't think: so. *(more laughter)* I often say to the Lord in my prayers (that) I want to be like Paul. I want to be an Apostle Paul. Here is a man that I covet.

(Comment: *What the manuscript cannot give are the inflections and intonations in Pastor Bonner's voice. It* *is so very obvious that the Apostle Paul is someone for whom our Bishop has great admiration and respect. And when Pastor talks about this Biblical legend of a saint, there is a lot of enthusiasm and excitement in his voice.)*

J.C.R., Jr.: I think maybe you touched on this earlier when we talked about the members being sometimes more spiritual than the pastor, but I will still ask this question. You state on page 77 that "every individual has the power to free another." Not just the minister but anyone who has the gift of the Holy Ghost. Is that what you were referring to when you said that some members can see farther that the minister?

Pastor Bonner: Yes.

J.C. R., Jr.: For a person who has accepted the Apostolic doctrine and gotten baptized (in water) in Jesus' Name, and then goes back to his/her former tradition and stops acknowledging it, what happens to that person?

Pastor Bonner: The Bible says they are not fit for the Kingdom.

J.C.R., Jr.: Hmm. OK. Alright. Now you mentioned, you actually spoke against celibacy as it applies to Roman Catholic priests and (nuns) sisters; but in the case of a saint (church member) male or female who has separated or divorced and that former spouse lives for ten or fifteen years after divorce so that the person is not free to remarry, isn't the end result the same as a priest and a nun? So how do you deal with that biblically in terms of one having to remain single and celibate?

Pastor Bonner: I have been single now for a number of years. I have been able to rise to levels since my wife passed on. I have been able to reach (spiritual) levels, that I never reached before. When she was alive, you know, I loved to make love. Now I make love to Jesus. I am in love with Jesus. I tell Him how much I love Him. I don't have a wife to tell her how much I love her. And yet I have the same capacity that I had when my wife was alive. So, I turn to Jesus instead of turning to women. I love women, I'm not funny (gay); and I want to be married. But I know once I marry it's going to interfere with my relationship with Jesus. I know this. When I get married... I'm going to give up some of this praying *(hearty laughter)*. You know Paul never married. He fell in love with Jesus. And he did not have divided affection *(more hearty laughter)*. Hallelujah!

J.C.R., Jr.: Can I ask my next question? I wanted to make sure that I didn't cut you off *(both laugh heartily)*.

Pastor Bonner: You've got to loose me now. *(very great laughter)*!!!

J.C.R., Jr.: On page 91, you were ministering in a prayer line—well let me read it. This is a quote. "During one anointing service, the Spirit gave me insight into many people who came before me. I found that I couldn't just pray for these people and let them go. I had to hold onto them and work with them a little longer so that the Spirit could do what it willed to do in giving those persons their blessing of liberty and deliverance."

Can you talk about exactly what happens when you are holding onto a person, while the Spirit is doing whatever He wants or needs to do?

Pastor Bonner: That's when a minister has the Spirit of discernment. You have got to be able to face the problems of the person, not just lay hands on them. You got to be able to see and the Lord will show you through the Spirit of discernment that this person wants to be delivered. So, hold to them awhile longer; pray with them a while longer. That's what that means.

J.C.R., Jr.: Alright, alright. Ah—I have a committee working with me doing the typing—and this question came up on pages 93-94. "Women have always been a thorn in God's flesh." What does that mean?

Pastor Bonner: Because God never knew a woman, never had a relationship with a woman; he created the man and the woman to have a relationship. So what God has to do is witness a man and a woman in the bed making love, something that He himself has never experienced. He just has to be an observer and just imagine what it is like, because He doesn't know what it is like to make love.

J.C.R., Jr.: That is awesome. I don't know if anyone else would have thought of that but you *(much laughter)*.

And now on page 97, this is a quote: "Jesus is not looking at your gifts but at your works." My question is aren't your gifts a part of your works?

Pastor Bonner: What does the Bible say about a man's works? (They) shall be tried by fire. If his works burn, he shall suffer long.

So, my works are not necessarily my gifts, because my works can burn, my gifts cannot bum.

J.C.R., Jr.: Pastor Bonner, I appreciate your taking time out of your very busy schedule to allow me this time and opportunity.

Pastor Bonner: It's my pleasure.
(End of Interview)

Chapter Seven
Armageddon

There is really no other title for this chapter other than the single word Armageddon. This is a word that seems to cause confusion in some, while giving hope to others. It possesses in a rather strange way, some intrigue and fascination; and it is a word pregnant with so many possibilities relative to Christian doctrine, one would categorize Armageddon as a part of the teachings in Eschatology, which is a focus on what we call "the last things."

Someone asked from whence do we get this word? Well in the sacred writings, it is found only one time; in Revelation 16: 16,

> And he gathered them together into a place called in the Hebrew tongue Armageddon.

Although there is only one biblical reference, a multiplicity of authors have written detailed books on the subject that purports to give us data about the extreme importance of Armageddon. Looking at the simplest definition, it means the location of the final battle between the forces of good and the forces of evil. Thus, according to one Christian viewpoint, the Battle of Armageddon is very critical, and requires our taking this whole issue very, very seriously. And, that is precisely what Pastor Bonner did when he wrote the book, *The Battle of Armageddon,* which was published in 1991. He said that the message for Armageddon is taken directly from a Gospel passage, Luke 21:36:

> Watch ye therefore, and pray always, that ye may be accounted worthy to escape all these things that shall come to pass, and to stand before the Son of Man.

As a part of the introduction in his book, we learn that Pastor Bonner wrote this shortly after the invasion of Kuwait by Iraq. That was during the presidential administration of the first President Bush (George Herbert Walker). The American military was joined by a coalition of United Nations troops in response to that act of aggression. Many were using the word Armageddon to describe this particular war; and, while he agreed that Armageddon would take place, the conflict in Kuwait was not it.

When reading the book, one is keenly aware that our Bishop has gone to great lengths to write a rather exhaustive chronicle showing what must and will precede the Battle of Armageddon. Look at these words:

> More than one third of the Bible is prophecy, and many scholars conclude that about half of those prophecies have already been fulfilled... This is what

makes the Bible such a forceful weapon against those who charge it to be just another book... Thus, according to the scriptures, the Battle of Armageddon cannot take place until specific events are accomplished first. These events include:

1. The Gathering of the Jewish People Back to Palestine

2. The Gospel preached in all the world (Matt 24)

3. The Rapture of the Church of Jesus Christ (I Thess 4: 13-18)

4. The Rise of the Antichrist and his ultimate domination of the world

5. The greater part of the Tribulation Period

6. The sealing of the 144,000 Jews[37]

It is his contention that some of these events have already occurred, such as the Jews began their return from

---

[37] William L. Bonner, *The Battle of Armageddon*. New York: Greater Refuge Temple Publisher, 1991, pp. 9-10.

Diaspora in 1948. That was the year in which the United Nations officially recognized a part of Palestine as the Middle Eastern republic of Israel. That act has also been a source of continuous conflict, because Arabs, Jews, and Palestinians have not stopped fighting in almost six decades. And while this ever-present war zone may have a clear latter-day agenda, those who teach about Armageddon see something that is far greater than the present repeated skirmishes.

Many who have studied critically, observed, and analyzed these historic events, point to a very basic view. A family dispute, over hundreds of years ago will have its conclusion in a mammoth global disaster. The family started with Abraham and Sarah in Genesis. In the book of beginnings,

God made a covenant with Abraham, who was known as Abram at that time (Genesis 15). But a major concern that the old patriarch had was the fact that he had no heir. Thus, in his way of thinking, no matter how great or plentiful the blessings that God would give him, there was no son, no child to inherit his wealth, and continue the legacy. Of course, the Almighty God was way ahead of Abram and had already prepared for his offspring to come on the scene.

What Abraham ran into though was a time line problem. When the Lord did not see fit that Sarah should get pregnant according to their thinking, this saintly old couple decided to intervene. That timeline has been a problem for so many believers down through the ages. So many have made commitments to God and vowed to serve Him no matter what. Many did not give up after a few weeks or months, but persisted and held on for years; all the while thinking, "Lord when are you going to answer? When will I hear from you? I mean this problem or that situation, has been weighing on me for a long time and I just need to hear from you Lord." In counseling with different individuals, most pastors have no idea how often those statements have been expressed. That time line problem has tried the faith and the patience of way too many.

The thing we must remember though is that God is never obligated to move by our timeline; for I truly believe that He has His own. It reminds me of a song that we used to sing in the Apostolic Church when I was growing up.

> You can't hurry God, You've got to trust and give Him time, no matter how long it takes. He is a God that you can't hurry; He will be there don't you worry. He may not come when you want Him, but He is always on time.

That song, in all of its simplicity, is a stark reminder that this universe inclusive of our individual concerns, is steadfastly in the hands of Almighty God. He is constantly aware as to what is confronting each of us; and I believe He already has the answers. The question is that time line, will we wait (while working) until the Lord answers or will we to, try to intercede?

That is exactly what Abraham and Sarah did. Looking at their chronological ages, and believing that the biological clock had ticked out, they sought an alternative that had not been approved by their Lord. Sarah temporarily delegated her duties as a wife to her servant, Hagar, who subsequently cohabitated with Abraham. From this union, Ishmael was born. All of the initial excitement and joy that generally accompanies the arrival of a newborn soon gave way to envy and strife. Hagar no longer saw herself as the maid in the "back house." After all, she had provided Abraham with something that Sarah had been unable to do, give him a son.

So, what was supposed to be a time for festive celebration ended up in the expulsion of Hagar and her son, Ishmael. But the story does not end there. Sarah did, in fact, have a son, Isaac, with Abraham, in spite of her advanced age of 90 years old. However, because of that timeline problem, needless and unsolicited, intervention created a family rift. And the descendants of Ishmael and Isaac have continued to feud for centuries and the fighting continues.

There is another part to this story though, Abraham later married another woman by the name of Keturah who had six sons with him. They were Zimran, Joksham, Midian, Medan, Ishbuk, and Shunah. Now these six, along with Ishmael, have really become historic enemies to Isaac. For he alone inherited the spiritual part of the covenant that God made with Abraham. The other seven were blessed in abundance as it pertained to economics. But they were not part of those great spiritual blessings given to Isaac and his descendants through Jacob.

The drama unfolds even more. Isaac and his wife, Rebekah, had twin sons, Jacob and Esau whose feud became legendary and totally unique. In their mother's womb, they were enlightened by the Spirit of God concerning their importance. These unborn infants engaged in "womb wrestling" so fierce that Rebekah sought relief, solace, and some answers from the Lord. She was at the breaking point, feeling as if she could not go on any longer. Can you just image what agony and pain she experienced! I find it difficult trying to conceptualize her plight. But it was the Lord who responded with exactly what she needed. In Genesis 25:23, He said:

> ... Two nations are in thou womb, and two manner of people shall be separated from thy bowels; and the one people shall be stronger than the other people; and the elder shall serve the younger.

This verse is very important, so let us do it over in a more modem translation. The former was from the King James Version. Please note:

And He told her, The sons in your womb shall become two rival nations. One will be stronger than the other; and the older shall be a servant of the younger.

One of the reasons that verse was so important at the time of Rebekah's pregnancy was that the older (or oldest) male child became the heir to everything that the father had. The birthright, if you will, belonged to the older sibling. That was the reason that this womb battle had been underway. And the uniqueness of it all was the battle of unborn siblings. God had endowed them with a level of knowledge and understanding that had gone counter to any pregnancy prior to Rebekah's. No other womb experience came close to being this remarkable until we get to the New Testament and read about John the Baptist being filled with the Holy Spirit in the womb of his mother, Elizabeth. The second and most awesome ever was the virgin birth of our Lord, by His precious servant, Mary.

God knows the end from the beginning. Even though Esau preceded Jacob out of the womb, the prophecy preceded both of them, and God said that the older would serve the younger. That meant that the Lord was changing the tradition as it related to "heir rights." While the Lord knew that Esau would be born first, His choice for the covenant blessing from Abraham and Isaac, was Jacob. Last time anyone checked, the Lord still has the right and prerogative to do whatever He wants, whenever He wants, and however He wants.

Not only was the tradition altered on this occasion by the Lord, but there was at least one other time when tradition was intentionally changed. When Jacob was well along in years, the Lord allowed him to be reunited with his son Joseph, when Jacob thought he was dead. In Genesis, chapter 48, Joseph brought his two sons to grandfather Jacob to be blessed. Again, focusing on tradition, Joseph placed his older son Manasseh, to the right of his grandfather, while placing Ephraim, the younger son, to Jacob's left. When he prepared to bless them, Jacob crossed his arms putting his right hand on Ephraim and his left hand on Manasseh. By so doing, the younger son received a greater blessing than the older son. Well, Joseph was so upset that he physically tried to change the hands of Jacob to fit the tradition. But his father said, "Joseph, I know what I am doing. Yes, Ephraim is the younger, but he will be a greater nation than his older brother Manasseh." Jacob went on to say that future generations of Israelites would pray to be blessed like Ephraim and Manasseh; putting the younger son's name first.

How did Jacob know to do this? Was he acting impulsively because he had gotten upset with Manasseh and was determined to punish him? Absolutely not!! Just as God, by His Spirit, spoke to Jacob and Esau in the womb of their mother, Rebekah, God also spoke to Jacob to let him know about the Divine Choice. Joseph's tradition said it was to be Manasseh; but God said *it will be* Ephraim.

Earlier I listed the six sons of Abraham born to him by his second wife, Keturah. It was also mentioned at that time that Ishmael was the very first son of Abraham by Sarah's maid, Hagar. As the elder, or this case, the oldest son, Ishmael, should have received that special blessing. But, as you recall, Sarah and Abraham circumvented the Lord to get the job done their own way. In spite of that, God did bless Ishmael in a mighty way; just not like Isaac. Note Genesis 17: 18-21:

> And Abraham said unto God, o that Ishmael might live before thee! And God said, Sarah thy wife shall bear thee a son indeed; and thou shalt call his name Isaac: and I will establish my covenant with him for an everlasting covenant, and with his seed after him. And as for Ishmael, I have heard thee: Behold, I have blessed him and will make him fruitful, and will multiply him exceedingly; twelve princes shall he beget and I will make him a great nation. But my

covenant will I establish with Isaac, which Sarah shall bear unto thee...

The Scriptures, as well as these contemporary times, remind us that God has blessed people who are outside of his covenant group repeatedly. But it has not meant, and does not mean, that those individuals and those nations will choose to serve and thank God for His bountifulness toward them. A case in point would be Ishmael. Oh, how the Lord blessed him. Just like the son of Isaac, Jacob became the father of twelve sons, Ishmael was given descendants from twelve princes. They were Kedeman, Naphish, Jetur, Tema, Hadar, Massa, Dumah, Mishma, Mibsam, Adbeel, Kedar, and Nebajoth.

Now if I correctly understand the teaching of the Bishop, these twelve descendants of Ishmael along with the six sons of Keturah all became enemies to the covenant people of God. He gives additional information about the enemies of God's people. This time a list of people who were the descendants of Esau referred to as Edom is shared. They are called dukes in Genesis 36:40-43. Timnah, Alvah, Jetheth, Aholibamah, Elah, Pinon, Kenaz, Teman, Mibzar, Magdiel, Iram. This list should be added to the ones previously stated to get an initial listing of the enemies of Jacob (Israel).

His point is this. The descendants of Ishmael, the sons of Keturah, and the descendants of Esau were all blessed by God. No, they were not a part of the covenant, but they were richly blessed by God. However, they consciously chose to become enemies to God's people. Being outside of the covenant did not exempt them from the opportunities to be saved. Their choice exempted them from salvation. In fact. like Caleb, Rahab, and Ruth, others outside of the covenant could have chosen to accept the Almighty God. In my opinion, it is very noteworthy that each of these three Gentiles made most inspiring contributions to the history of God's people, while becoming a part of the covenant themselves.

Of the three, I have always found Rahab's acknowledgment of Israel's God to be faith inspiring. She recognized that the god of Jericho could never do for them what Jehovah had done for Israel. By demonstrating this kind of faith in Almighty God, not only was she and her family spared, she also became a part of the covenant people.

Ruth, on the other hand, presents to us quite a phenomenal story of sacrificing. We all know that a committed life with the Lord entails sacrifice as a part of the journey. Well, we can only speculate about the awesome example that Naomi lived in front of Ruth, a Moabite. I say that because while Orpah, the other daughter-in-law of Naomi, chose to stay in Moab with her kindred, Ruth did just the opposite. Please imagine the enormous sacrifice that Ruth freely made by leaving her natural country. Her father, mother, relatives, customs, and traditions could not influence her from going with

Naomi. Thus, one can surmise that the godly life that her mother-in-law lived in front of Ruth was just too much for her to resist. Staying in Moab and practicing the religion there obviously did not compare to what Ruth had seen in Naomi. Consequently, Ruth gathered what she had or what she needed and went with Naomi back to her house in Bethlehem. Keep in mind, Ruth was not just accepting Naomi, she was in fact accepting the Almighty God that Naomi served. This decision enabled Ruth to become a part of God's covenant people.

Then we come to Caleb who was born and reared as a Kenezite. But yet he became as Yahweh's servant; not the god of the Kenezites. And who in scripture gives any greater example of what it means to trust in God categorically and unconditionally? His greatest blessing was held up for forty years; not because of lack of faith or disobedience. The folk with whom he was associated, the covenant people, had expressed doubt in God. And He took forty years to raise up a new generation of believers, while allowing a generation of believers to die in the wilderness. And through it all, Caleb never wavered in his faith in Yahweh. Rather he chose to become a believing covenant follower.

My point is simply this. Anyone who was not born into God's covenant family could still choose to become a part. Unlike Rahab, Ruth, and Caleb, way too many others chose to be numbered among the enemies of God and His people. Let me I add though, that God always punishes His enemies at the appropriate times. However, this situation involving Caleb is a glaring instance of how He chastises the covenant people.

Today, though, many of the Arab nations are the descendants of Ishmael. And, because they seem unwilling to reconsider their positions, they have become a part of historical prophecy helping to set the stage for that final battle between the forces for God and forces against God.

Another aspect of Armageddon revolves around the sons of Noah. Shem, Ham, and Japheth. Again, according to the teachings of Pastor Bonner, each of these sons became the progenitor of major races. Ham was the forefather of the Blacks or the Negroids, Japheth was the forefather of the Whites or Caucasoids, and Shem was the father to Asians or Mongoloids.

In his teachings, Pastor Bonner contends that the ten nations of the European Common Market are a contemporary part of Japheth's descendants. These countries include France, Germany, Italy, Holland, Belgium, Luxemburg, Greece, Great Britain, Ireland, and Denmark. Now if you direct your attention to the book of Daniel, chapter two, made up of Iron and Clay is composed of ten nations. It is the belief of Pastor Bonner that these contemporary nations are the latter-day representatives and the fulfillment of that prophecy. Notice what he said on this issue:

This will comprise the 10 nations (European Common Market) which are represented in Daniel, chapter 2... The antichrist will emerge from one of these ten (10) kingdoms. He will first lead his own nation, then he will be given power from (or by) all the rest.[38]

The previously stated enemies along with the descendant nations of Noah's sons cover the majority of nations in existence today. And the citizens in every one of these nations will have the opportunity to be saved. However, in many, the governmental leadership will align themselves with those who are against the Lord Jesus Christ. The leader in all of this will be the antichrist.

As a way of showing or helping us to better prepare and understand the coming of the antichrist, Pastor Bonner shares with us what he calls <u>Characteristics of the Antichrist.</u>

Rather than give all of the scriptures that he has put together, I will just list one scripture with each characteristic and recommend that you obtain a personal copy of his book. Please note the following:

1. He shall be a Jew.

There is disagreement amongst biblical scholars whether he will be a Jew or Gentile. When we look at

---

[38] Ibid., p. 97.

Daniel 11: 37, there is a definite reference to the 'God of his fathers' showing God in a capitalized form. As Greek scholars translated the Bible from Hebrew to Greek, they always capitalized God if they were referring to Jehovah God. Neither shall he regard the God of his fathers, nor the desire of women, nor regard any god: for he shall magnify himself above all.

2. *Some believe he (Antichrist) will not only be a Jew, but will come from the Tribe of Dan.*

In Revelation, chapter 7, where the 12,000 from each tribe is mentioned to comprise the 144,000, the Tribe of Joseph is substituted for Dan. Because of this omission, (and God never makes a mistake) many believe that the Antichrist shall come from the Tribe of Dan. (Revelation 7:4) And I heard the number of them which were sealed: and there were sealed an hundred and forty and four thousand of all the tribes of the children of Israel.

3. *He will be an intellectual genius.* Daniel 8:24-25

Toward the end of their kingdoms, when they have become morally rotten, an angry king shall rise to power with great shrewdness and intelligence. His power shall be mighty, but it will be satanic strength, and not his own. Prospering wherever he turns, he will destroy all who oppose him, though their armies be mighty, and he will devastate God's people.

4. ***He will be an oratorical genius.*** Daniel 11:36

The king will do exactly as he pleases, claiming to be greater than every god there is, even blaspheming the God of gods, and prospering until his time is up.

5. ***He will be a political genius.*** Revelation 17:14-15

Together they will wage war against the Lamb, and the Lamb will conquer them; for his is Lord over all lords, and King of kings, and his people are the called and chosen and faithful ones. The oceans, lakes and rivers that the woman is sitting on represent masses of people of every race and nation.

6. ***He will be a commercial genius.*** Revelation 13:17

And that no man might buy or sell, save he that had the mark, or the name of the beast, or the number of his name.

7. ***He will be a military genius.*** Revelation 13:2

This creature looked like a leopard but had bear's feet and a lion's mouth! And the Dragon gave him his own power and throne and great authority.

8. *He will manipulate many people to worship him.* II Thessalonians 2:4

He will defy every god there is, and tear down every other object of adoration and worship. He will go in and sit as God in the temple of God, claiming that he himself is God. Revelation 13:8. And all that dwell upon the earth shall worship him, whose names are not written in the book of life of the Lamb slain from the foundation of the world.

9. *He will begin by controlling the Western Power Block of Nations.* Revelation 17: 12 & 13

His ten horns are ten kings who have not yet risen to power; they will be appointed to their kingdoms for one brief moment, to reign with him. They will all sign a treaty giving them power and strength to him.

10. *He will make a seven-year covenant with Israel but will break it after three and a half years.* Daniel 9:27

This king will make a seven-year treaty with the people, but after half that time, he will break his pledge and stop the Jews from all their sacrifices and their offerings; then, as a climax to all his terrible deeds, the Enemy shall utterly defile the Sanctuary of God. But in God's time and plan, his judgment will be poured out upon this Evil One.

11. **_He will attempt to destroy all of Israel during the latter 3 1/2 years of the Tribulation Period._** Revelation 12:14

But she was given two wings like those of a great eagle, to fly into the wilderness to the place prepared for her, where she was cared for and protected from the Serpent, the Dragon for three and a half years.

12. **_He will destroy the false religious systems so that he may rule unhindered_** Revelation 17:16

The scarlet animal and his ten horns—which represent ten kings who will reign with him. All hate the woman and will attack her and leave her naked and ravaged by fire.[39]

13.**_He will set himself up as God._** Daniel 11:37
Neither shall he regard the God of his fathers, no should be praised r the desire of women, nor regard any god: for he shall magnify himself above all.

---

[39] (i.e., women dressed in scarlet and purple representing false Christianity - Post Rapture Religious groups - Revelation 17 Who attempt to intermingle and fellowship with the Beast. (Mixing Religion with Government) For her fornication and whoring, she is destroyed by the Antichrist himself.

14. **_He will be the first creature thrown into the lake of fire._** Revelation 19:20

And the beast was taken and with him the false prophet that wrought miracles before him with which he deceived them that had received the mark of the beast, and them that worshipped his image. These both were cast alive into a lake of fire burning with brimstone.

    This entire list of characteristics of the Antichrist was taken from the book by Pastor Bonner, *The Battle of Armageddon*, pages 100-106.

    Other very insightful parts of the book include *The Five-Fold Purpose of The Battle of Armageddon* (page 57), and *Judgment of the Hypocrites Who Have Taught Another Gospel* (page 60).

    Beginning with page 68, he titles Section II as *The Events of The Battle of Armageddon*. In compiling these, one column gives us the sequential unfolding of events, while the second column provides scriptural references that validate these events. This section also reminds us who the <u>Major Actors for Armageddon will be.</u> You find that, beginning on page 76.

    Reading the Bishop's teaching on Armageddon has certainly reignited my interest in this subject from its dormancy. While many ministries have a primary focus on individual and corporate salvation in the local assembly, there is a need for more. Writings on Armageddon provide a viewpoint that shows some world situations fulfilling prophetic mandates in the Holy Bible. Perhaps there should be much more instructions on this subject in a far greater number of churches. If we are closer to a major cataclysmic event on earth that will have profound implications for the church and the world, then more needs to be communicated in our pulpits. And when I say "communicated," I don't mean so many simply declaring that "Jesus is coming back soon." I am talking about the need for the leadership in many churches across the world to inform the followership about these critical and very germane issues.

Is it, for example, coincidental that many in the Islamic world appear to have unadulterated hatred for Israel, the United States of America, and parts of Western Europe? Has there been anything in the foreign policy decisions of these countries that have been blatantly unfair to Arab nations in particular, and nations of color in general? Or is it that the terrorist attacks on those are really just a part of the Divinely scripted plan designated to usher us toward the Battle of Armageddon? What role do we give to the oil producing nations? Obviously, there is a great need for many more followers of our Lord Jesus Christ to spend time in prayer and instruction delving into the richness and depth of this subject matter. Only then will we be able to grasp, in a significant way, the meaning of these events as propagated by the proponents of the Armageddon doctrine.

Conclusion
Stay On Course

Even though I was alive during the last fifteen years of his life, it was never my privilege to meet the renown and legendary Bishop Robert Clarence Lawson. As a youth barely in my teens, I do recall my father talking about him. His comments always reflected a high level of respect and admiration, and, as it turned, out my father did have a historical connection to Bishop Lawson.

In 1931, Dad got saved at the St. Peter's Church of God (Apostolic) in Winston-Salem, NC. It was on Easter Sunday night, and a co-worker of his had repeatedly invited him to visit St. Peter's pastored by Bishop Eli Neal. After having attended his own church for Easter Sunday morning service (Mt. Zion Missionary Baptist Church also in Winston-Salem), Dad accepted the invitation to visit St. Peter's. Subsequent to hearing the powerful message by Bishop Neal, he went forward in response to the altar call. That very night he got baptized in water in the name of our Lord Jesus Christ, and as he was coming up out of the water Dad began speaking in tongues, as he received the baptism of the Holy Spirit.

His pastor, Bishop Eli Neal, was also the presiding bishop of the Church of God Apostolic at that time. But Neal's predecessor, Bishop Thomas J. Cox, had organized the national church in Danville, Kentucky in 1897. At that time, though, it was not Apostolic. However, somewhere around 1914, or 1915, Bishop Cox heard the oneness message preached by Bishop R. C. Lawson, and then got baptized in the name of the Lord Jesus Christ and also received the Holy Ghost. Not too long after that, the national church name was changed from the Christian Faith Band to the Church of God (Apostolic), incorporated and 1919 in Paris, Ky. Like the originators of my father's home organization, many early Apostolic leaders were touched in some way by Bishop R. C. Lawson. He was obviously used by the Lord to minister to a lot of people who never became a part of the Church of Our Lord Jesus Christ.

In his book titled, *My Father in The Gospel*, Pastor Bonner spoke with so much love about his wonderful father, Bishop Lawson. Additional comments about him can be found in the booklet, Stay On Course and Add Thou To It. To Pastor Bonner and so many, many others, Bishop Lawson was "a man of integrity, dedication, and consecration, with an immense intellectual capacity." Continuing, Pastor informs us that Bishop Lawson had great wisdom and knowledge.

No doubt one of the outstanding characteristics about Bishop Lawson was his acceptance in ecumenical religious circles. Yes, he was totally grounded in the Apostolic doctrine, not wavering at all. Yet his message from the Lord was so powerful and anointed that persons in other denominations sought him out frequently. There were even pastors from other denominational groups who were led by God to come with their entire congregations and affiliate with Bishop Lawson.

One of the areas in which Pastor received great blessings from Bishop Lawson was while serving as his chauffeur. This gave father and son significant, quality time to dialogue about a variety of subjects. This also gave Pastor Bonner a very special time to glean choice nuggets of wisdom from Bishop Lawson, and it was also during this time that he became determined to be blessed by his father the way the biblical prophet Elisha was blessed by his mentor, Elijah.

During this period Pastor Bonner was not only a spiritual son, at times he really became a son to Bishop Lawson in every sense of the word. Perhaps it was because of this bond that Pastor Bonner recognized vividly the joy and pain that his father went through. One could justifiably conclude that the hurt, pain, grief, and anguish reached its zenith in 1957. That was when the Church of Our Lord Jesus Christ went through a major split. The primary reason for the piercing level of agony experienced by Bishop Lawson was the fact that the split was led by his spiritual sons, Bishop Smallwood Williams, Bishop John Beane, and Bishop Joseph Moore who were three of the five bishops on the board of the initial Bible Way Church Worldwide, the resulting splinter group. And, as was said earlier, most believed that Bishop Smallwood Williams was the heir apparent to Bishop Lawson as presider of COOLJC. It was after these events that Bishop Lawson uttered those now sacred words, don't tear apart what the Lord had used him to build up. Just simply, "Add Thou To It."

In his booklet, *Stay on Course*, Pastor Bonner talked in specific details precisely how he had tried to do just that. It is indeed a fact that during the tenure of Pastor Bonner as the presider and later chief apostle, the Church of Our Lord Jesus Christ has grown in a mighty way. Among predominantly Black Apostolic (Oneness Pentecostal) groups, it is probably the second largest; with only Pentecostal Assemblies of the World exceeding it. As we all know, PAW is the mother of contemporary Apostolic church organizations.

Upon stepping down as the presiding apostle in 1995, Bishop Bonner shared "wisdom vital to the future success of the Church of Our Lord Jesus Christ." The future chief apostle encouraged them to stand for the Gospel without compromising. He also said:

> We are distinguished by the standard that we have. We are also distinguished by the anointing that the Lord gives to the Presiding Apostle ... We must never lose the image and likeness of the glory and power of Jesus that rest upon the Church of Our Lord Jesus

Christ... I say to you that we are highly favored ... The Lord has been with us.

Pastor Bonner continued his very inspiring comments by saying:

> I have suffered tremendously mentally and physically ... (but) I do not regret my pain or my suffering. To God be the glory, honor and praise.[40]

In closing his remarks, Pastor Bonner raised an issue that he feels very strongly about; the role of women in the Church of Our Lord Jesus Christ. He stated:

> We must not change our doctrinal position as it relates to men, women, or anything pertaining to the gospel of Jesus Christ... This was handed down to us (by the Apostles), and we must preserve the right order of truth... The women, by their sheer numbers will influence the rise and fall of the Church. The women will influence whether we will be a true Pentecostal body or whether we will compromise and succumb to doctrines and other religious teachings.[41]

---

[40] William L. Bonner. *Stay On Course and Add Thou To It.* 1995, s.l., s.n., p. 6.

[41] Ibid., pp. 6-7

to not wear those titles in name only. Never lose the dedication and commitment that goes with the offices. For each title is accompanied by an appropriate level of responsibility. Be as willing to accept the job description as you are to seek and accept the title. That alone qualifies each of them to be leaders in COOLJC. The Chief Apostle closed by saying:

> I just want you young people, missionaries, pastors, and evangelists to remember to preserve what the Lord has given to the Church of Our Lord Jesus Christ lest we become just another institution. I beseech you to stay on course. [42]

---

[42] Ibid., p. 9.

Bibliography

Bonner, William L. *The Doctrinal Guide of The Solomon's Temple, Detroit MI: Solomon's Temple: s.n.*

_____. *The Apostolic Dilemma.* New York: Greater Refuge Temple Publisher, 1976.

_____. *The Apostolic Dilemma Volume Two, Women's Liberation,* New York: Greater Refuge Temple Publisher, 1976.

_____. *Three Women: Sarah - Rebecca - Jezebel.* New York: Greater Refuge Temple Publisher, 1993

_____. *The Uncontrolled Emotions of Saved Young People.* New York: Greater Refuge Temple Publisher, 1977.

_____. *Another Comforter. Detroit, MI*: s.n., 1978.

_____. *Life in the Holy Spirit.* New York: Greater Refuge Temple Publisher, 1983.

_____. *The Battle of Armageddon.* New York: Greater Refuge Temple Publisher, 1991

_____. *Stay On Course and Add Thou To It.* s.l., s.n., 1995

_____. *My Father in The Gospel: Bishop R. C. Lawson.* New York: Greater Refuge Temple, 1979.

_____. *Take This Guarantee And Run With It!* s.l., s.n., s.d.

_____. *Southern Pines Seminar '92.* s.l., s.n., s.d.

_____. *And the High Places I'll Bring Down: Bishop William L Bonner, The Man and His God.* Detroit, MI: W. L. Bonner Literary Committee, 1999.

Appendices

The Church of Our Lord Jesus Christ
Board of Apostles

Bishop William L. Bonner, Chief Apostle

Bishop James 1. Clark, Jr., Presiding Apostle

Bishop Matthew Norwood, Vice Presiding Apostle

Bishop Robert Sanders, Vice Presiding Apostle

Bishop Gentle Groover, Exec Assistant to the Chief Apostle, and Past Presiding Apostle

Bishop Bradford Betty

Bishop Walter Jackson

Bishop James Maye

Bishop Henry Moultrie

Bishop Samuel Peters

Bishop Fred Rubin

Bishop Wesley Taylor

Churches Pastored by Bishop Bonner

Solomon's Temple
2341 East 7 Mile Road Detroit,
MI 48234

Greater Refuge Temple
2081 Adam C. Powell, Jr. Boulevard
New York, NY 10027
(Mother Church/International Headquarters of The Church of Our Lord Jesus Christ)

Refuge Temple
4456 Medgar Evers Blvd
Jackson, Miss. 39213

Refuge Temple
470 56th Street NE
Washington, DC 20019

Refuge Temple
4450 Argent Court
Columbia, SC 29203
(Southern Regional Headquarters of The Church of Our Lord Jesus Christ)

www.ingramcontent.com/pod-product-compliance
Lightning Source LLC
LaVergne TN
LVHW041334080426
835512LV00006B/456